CLASSIC FRESHWATER FISH COOKING

By Eileen Clarke

Voyageur Press

Edited by Michael Dregni
Series design by Andrea Rud
Printed in the United States of America

98 99 00 01 02   5 4 3 2 1

Library of Congress Cataloging-in-Publication Data
Clarke, Eileen.
      Classic freshwater fish cooking / by Eileen Clarke.
          p.   cm. — (The fish and game kitchen)
      Includes index.
      ISBN 0-89658-345-7
      1. Cookery (Fish)   2. Freshwater fishes.   I. Title.   II. Series.
    TX747.C6197   1998
    641.6′92—dc21   97–28582
                                                       CIP

Distributed in Canada by Raincoast Books, 8680 Cambie Street, Vancouver, B.C. V6P 6M9

Published by Voyageur Press, Inc.
123 North Second Street, P.O. Box 338, Stillwater, MN 55082 U.S.A.
612-430-2210, fax 612-430-2211

Educators, fundraisers, premium and gift buyers, publicists, and marketing managers: Looking for creative products and new sales ideas? Voyageur Press books are available at special discounts when purchased in quantities, and special editions can be created to your specifications. For details contact the marketing department at 800-888-9653.

CONTENTS

A fly fisherman works Oregon's Crooked River following a snowfall (Photo © Dennis Frates)

INTRODUCTION

Let's start by not being put off by the words "classic recipes" since all "classic" really means is that the recipe works. These are time-tested and trusted friends that have never failed, whether it was an informal Saturday afternoon at the lake or Sunday dinner with Grandma and Aunt Evelyn. Meal after meal, these recipes have warmed the hearts and bodies of people of all walks of life—and continents. They are not fads or fancies, nor are they made with hard-to-find and hard-to-handle ingredients, but recipes that have gained their reputations the old-fashioned way: being cooked, successfully, by ace and nimrod alike.

From Panfish Chips to New England–Style Perch Chowder to Beer Batter Fillets to Alder-Smoked Salmon, we have all lifted the fork and spoon and know these dishes as well as we know the back of our hands. In the past, however, some of us have depended on others—catalogs, restaurants, fabled grizzled veterans of the mysterious art of fish cookery—for recipes and shortcuts that added little more than fat and salt to the healthful fish we pulled from the water. No more. It's time to take control of those pails, stringers, creels, and live wells and learn a few old tricks all over again, this time streamlining the work a bit. You don't need to be in the kitchen all day to make chowder, or search all over the world for special ingredients, and these pages prove it.

While we're at it, I'll share a new way of filleting pike that I learned last fall fishing Fort Peck Lake in Montana. At first I was skeptical, thinking we would waste more fillet this way than we would gain. But home again, I took two fish of the same size and tested the new against the old: the results will amaze you. You will get big, solid, pike fillets, not the ribbons that have frustrated you before. We'll demystify that ancient art of knife sharpening, then find the best way to freeze fish, not just by guess and milk carton, but scientifically, with temperature-per-pound information you can use in your own freezer.

So let's start. Forget the fads and folderols. Let's explore an ancient world full of flavor and reliability. And find new old ways to enjoy the bounty of our lakes, rivers, and streams.

Fly fishing at sunrise on Washington's Lake Lenore (Photo © Dennis Frates)

Freezers and Microwaves: The Angler's Other Best Friends

Over the years, a lot of things have earned the title: "The Angler's Best Friend." Husbands and wives; Labrador retrievers and springer spaniels; lures and flies; knives and metal-clipped fillet planks; cough lozenges; motors, nets, waders, shoes, magnifying glasses for the aging baby boomers, and felt soles for mossy-bottomed streams. If I have forgotten some miracle of modern chemistry or classic oldie of ancient invention, I apologize. There are too many items, both bigger and smaller than a bread box, that vie for the angler's attention these days. In truth, a hook and something to camouflage the hook is all you need to get the fish—and if we ate the fish there, with our bare hands, sushi-style, or with fire, that would be the end of the list.

But how many of us live by the side of a good fishery, have time to catch our three squares three times a day, and would be happy eating one local fish forever? Or would want to be out there on a frigid day in December, with the wind blowing and the sleet driving harsh against our faces? If you are like me, you would put up with days like that for an elk or whitetail hunt, but prefer your fishing adventures be less arduous. Thus we do enjoy the summer afternoons in a walleye boat, spring in bass country, fall chasing the Neanderthal pike, July evenings camping by a lake with a bellyful of panfish dusted with cornmeal and fried hot in a bit of butter.

What is wrong then, with filling up the live well, the creel, or the cooler with a pile of delicate-tasting walleye, firm white-fleshed pike, or that gallivanting son of the south, bass? And how would you make that fresh taste of summer last—to enjoy some cold winter night—were it not for the freezer? Hail freezer! And hail, too, microwave, for those nights when we get home tired and hungry and realize we didn't take anything out of the freezer for dinner. To steal a page from sportswriters everywhere, I'd name the freezer and microwave the two most undervalued players in the angling world. And the least known.

The Freezer: Temperature, Style, and Capacity

Let's start with three easy questions about an appliance we all use several times a week. What temperature is your freezer operating at? Is your freezer efficient at keeping a stable temperature? And last, how much fish should you freeze at one time?

The first question is easy to answer. If you don't own a freezer/refrigerator thermometer, you should buy one. Why? Because there is a direct relationship between the temperature at which your freezer operates and how long you can successfully freeze a package of food. The goal is to have a sufficiently cold temperature, consistently maintained, freezing a well-wrapped package. The sufficient temperature is 0°Fahrenheit (−17.8° Celsius); the consistent maintenance of temperature comes from not opening the freezer often and having a chest freezer.

Fly fishing following a Montana springtime snowstorm (Photo © Alan and Sandy Carey)

At that optimum temperature, you can store fatty fish like salmon two to four months; trout four to six; and lower-fat fish like walleye and pike for six to eight months. This assumes that the fish was cleaned and put on ice immediately, and frozen—in a home freezer, at 0°F (−17.8°C)—within twenty-four hours of being caught. If you are fortunate enough to fish near a commercial flash freezer, the fish will last as much as 50 percent longer in your freezer.

Have you stuck that thermometer in your freezer yet? Take the test one step further: Let the thermometer sit in the center of the freezer for thirty minutes, then open the door and see how long it takes for the mercury to start rising. I just took a quick check of our three freezers. The two chest freezers in the laundry room and basement registered −5°F and 0°F (−20.5 and −17.8°C), respectively; the one above the refrigerator registered 10°F (−12.2°C). My Lab and I camped out over the open chest freezers for four minutes before we both got bored; the temperature never budged. (Druzilla is young, and she believes in the pheasant fairy—who will one day make all the birds in the freezer fly again just for her—so she's pretty intrigued with staring into the freezer.)

On the other hand, the freezer over the refrigerator took fifteen seconds to start warming with its door open. An upright freezer may operate at 0°F (−17.8°C) as easily as a chest freezer—as long as the door is closed—but because of its upright stance, it suffers the same quick temperature rise as your refrigerator's freezer compartment. It's a simple law of physics: cold air falls. Open any vertical unit and the frigid air falls like a lead balloon; open a chest freezer and that ancient law works to keep your food at a constant, efficient temperature. That seems worth the extra floor space it takes.

Efficient maintenance of temperature also depends on how full your freezer is. An empty freezer takes more energy to maintain temperature and a longer time to regain optimum temperature after you close the door again. That doesn't mean you need to keep every fish you catch to keep your freezer working efficiently. To take up space, you can fill milk jugs with water—and then take them along on hot summer days for a really cold, refreshing drink.

There is also a wide range of sizes and shapes in chest freezers—from single digit to mega-footage. We once had a 23-cubic-foot (690-cc) freezer, but replaced it with two 15-cubic-foot (450-cc) units. What we found was that it was better to have two smaller freezers than one large one. We keep one in the basement, for long-term

freezing; everything new goes in there, and it is opened four to five times a year. The upstairs freezer is for current use, and we dive into it two to four times a week for meals. Then we use our refrigerator/freezer for short-term, frequent-visit freezing, such as two to three weeks worth of fish and game meats, no more.

How Much Can You Freeze at One Time?

The answer to this question is a ratio between temperature and the volume of your freezer. First, remember that the faster you can freeze any food item, the longer it will last, and the better it will both look and taste—which is why a commercial flash-freezer affords you up to 50 percent more freezer life than a home unit. For the quickest freezing at home, follow this simple rule: At 0°F (−17.8°C), freeze only 1½ pounds (¾ kg) of fish for each 1 cubic-foot (30 cc) of freezer space. A 15-cubic-foot (450-cc) freezer, for instance, will freeze 22 pounds (10 kg) of fish quickly; a combined 30-cubic-foot (900-cc) freezer—as at our house—will freeze 45 pounds (20 kg). Measure your freezer's cubic footage, check its temperature, and then calculate your maximum.

It is also important not to stack the fish packages. Instead, place them in hanging baskets against the sides of the freezer, or atop other packages of already frozen items—always in a single layer. Hanging baskets (or oven shelves propped up on either end) allow for the best circulation of cold air around the entire package and the quickest freezing time.

While you should operate the freezer at 0°F (−17.8°C), when you know you are about to freeze a bunch of fish, it will help speed the process if you temporarily crank the temperature control as far down as it goes. Then, when everything is frozen solid, you can organize your walleye fillets in one sack, all your pike steaks in another, then turn the control back to autopilot: 0°F (−17.8°C).

Wrapping: Paper or Plastic?

In packaging, there are two things that limit freezer life. First is the fat content of the fish, which you can do nothing about. The second is trapped air, which you can do something about. Whether you use paper or plastic, work at pressing, vacuuming, or displacing as much air as possible out of your package to extend the freezer life of your catch.

Wrapping Fillets and Steaks

Some cookbooks recommend that 2- to 4-pound (1- to 2-kg) fish should be filleted, whereas larger fish should

Placing a fly (Photo © Alan and Sandy Carey)

be made into steaks and smaller ones frozen and cooked whole. On the other hand, a 4-pound (2-kg) salmon is one of the most popular fish to barbecue whole, and most families make their fish-cutting decisions based on what they would rather eat, instead of what some book tells them is proper. Personally, I think a steak is a beautiful thing, but I know lots of people who think steaks are only for four-legged creatures that moo. Read the books, think about what the "experts" say, then cut the fish up the way you want. More important than what it looks like, is what it tastes like.

Cut the steaks 1 to $1\frac{1}{2}$ inches ($2\frac{1}{2}$ to 4 cm) thick, and cut them from fish that will give you a steak at least 3 inches ($7\frac{1}{2}$ cm) across. Fillets should be about the same thickness, but in reality are thick on one end, then thin out toward the tail. To protect those thin ends from freezer burn, try stacking two fillets on top of each other, the thin end of one stacked on the thick end of the other. Then lay each pair on a piece of waxed paper and stack the pairs in 1- to 2-pound ($\frac{1}{2}$- to 1-kg) packages, depending on the size of your family. Or, if the fillets are thin to begin with, lay 1 to 2 pounds ($\frac{1}{2}$ to 1 kg) of them on a length of plastic wrap, with half the thin ends paired with half the thick ends for a uniformly

thick package. Then roll the fillets into a compact tube and press the air out of the sides of the package. Twist the ends, tuck them under, and wrap in freezer paper.

Stack the steaks the same way. But if you're making packages of four or more steaks, make two stacks side by side. It's the outer surface that gets freezer burned first, so the larger the package—still suiting the size of your family—with the least outer surface of flesh exposed, the better the protection for delicate flavors and textures. Think haystacks: It's always a wonder to me, in the middle of winter, to watch a rancher take bales from his haystack. All the exposed edges of the outer bales are brown and weathered—but all the inner bales are as fresh and green as the day they were stacked.

Wrapping Whole Fish

I often keep whole fish, sometimes to stuff, but mostly just because I don't know what I'll want to do with them three months down the road. And usually the whole fish I keep are longer than a bread box. Their irregular shapes make them a bit of a puzzle to wrap, but there are at least two ways that work.

The oldest method I know is to clean and rinse the fish, then wrap it tightly in plastic wrap, squeezing out all the air you can, then wrapping it snugly in foil or freezer paper. Or, you can wrap the fish in waxed paper, then seal it in foil or freezer paper. The problem, of course, is that with a whole fish as with whole birds, no matter how carefully you squeeze the air out, you cannot remove the air within the body cavity. Whole walleye are especially problematic, since their rib cage is so widely bowed.

If you like to keep whole fish, the solution may be the new vacuum seal units, which suck all the air out of a plastic bag and then seal it. A friend from Florida, who fishes a lot more days per year than I can in Montana, takes his vacuum sealer with him on trips so he can process and freeze his fish on the spot. I bought one this year because he's the most dedicated fisherman I know, and he really likes to cook. He bought one because one of his friends swore by it. That's how classic ideas get started.

The sealer could also replace the old milk carton gambit, or filling a resealable plastic bag with small fish parts, then topping it with water and gently pressing the air out. The problem with those methods has always been that the packaging water is inevitably absorbed into the flesh to some degree or another, depending on how quickly the package was frozen and thawed. The vacuum sealer's advantage is that you need not add water to protect the fish, which means when you thaw it three to nine months later, the fish is fresh and moist, and hasn't had the ghost of a chance of taking on any extraneous water, both things that affect the texture and taste of the finished product.

If you are only keeping a few fish, for under three months, about any method of wrapping will do; but the more fish you keep and the longer they stay in the freezer, the more attention you need to pay to trapped water and air.

Thawing:
Countertop, Refrigerator, or Microwave

The trouble with any freezer, like any machine, is the nut behind the wheel. You can have a freezer full of wonderful game, but if you forget to thaw it out for dinner, you may end up eating more commercial meat, or overprocessing your fish in the microwave.

The best and safest method for thawing any fish is to place it in the refrigerator, allowing approximately 8 hours for each 1 pound ($\frac{1}{2}$ kg). So a 3-pound ($1\frac{1}{2}$-kg) package of fillets will need to be taken out of the freezer 24 hours before you want to cook it—or about the time

you start dinner the night before. Whole fish take less time, for the same reason that they are more liable to be freezer burned: because there's a lot more surface area exposed to the air. (To compare: a whole chicken which is similar in shape to a whole fish thaws out at the rate of two hours for each pound/$\frac{1}{2}$ kg.)

Right, you say. The last thing I think about when I'm cooking dinner is tomorrow night's dinner. Well, there are shortcuts, and the microwave is only one.

Is there anything that has made the freezer-dependent angler's life easier than the microwave? Still, there is a tendency for all of us to think of the microwave as being a lot more powerful—and at the same time less powerful—than it really is. That's why we keep trying to cook a potato in less than four minutes, and why we resent it when we end up with cooked edges on fish we're thawing. Nothing can be all things to all foods.

So how do you thaw fish in a microwave without cooking it? Start with the timer. Instead of setting it for how long you think it will take to thaw your fish, microwave in steps. Set the timer for 1 minute at a time for 500-watt units; 40 seconds for 700-watt units. Then open the door and actually feel all around the package. If it is still cold, continue the 1-minute (or 40-second) regimen, turning the package over each time. Once it feels warm, you need to let the package sit in the microwave 3 to 4 minutes until it cools down, then process 1 minute (or 40 seconds) at a time again. Stop thawing when the package of fillets or steaks is thawed on the outside, but perhaps still somewhat frozen on the inside. Open the package and cut the fillets into individual serving sizes, or gently pull the pieces apart. (If you are going to deep-fry the fish, it must be completely thawed. You can lift or cut free the thawed sections and return the still-frozen section to the microwave.)

When thawing whole fish in the microwave, proceed as for fillets, but test for warmth at the tail; if the tail gets warm to the touch, you need to let it cool down before proceeding.

Microwaving to thaw fish, even when done slowly and carefully, still does not allow enough time for bacteria and germs to grow, as can happen if you thawed the fish on the counter. So it is both quick and safe—but it still has one problem.

While it has been a short time since microwaves first appeared, there has been an amazing evolution in their features. You may own a microwave that has anywhere from 400 to 900 watts, with one speed or ten, temperature sensors, carousels, delayed cooking, electronic control panels that belong on a space ship, or one knob with unreliable timing control. (I have the last; I believe that appliances touted as a convenience should be just that.) In general, you can boil water at 700 watts, bake muffins and cook rice at 360; 245 is recommended for defrosting, which is obviously considered a delicate operation, since softening ice cream occurs at only a slightly lower wattage.

Slowly thawed fish loses less of its natural moisture and remains more delicate in texture than fish thawed quickly. The best way to thaw fish still is letting it sit overnight in the refrigerator. When you need to microwave, use the appliance delicately, slowly, and with frequent rests. The oven may be high-tech, but fish are still part of the natural world.

One more technical note: I own two microwaves. The smaller one stays on the kitchen counter for everyday use; the larger one in the pantry for thawing large roasts. The "large" one is not only larger in size, but is a 700-watt unit, compared to the "small" 500-watt unit. Over the years, I've discovered that, brownouts and power outages aside, a cup of water boils in 3 minutes at 500 watts and 2 minutes at 700 watts. In other words, 200 watts additional power cuts cooking time by more than 30 percent.

With all the varieties of microwaves on the market, the best advice is to proceed slowly, and touch the baby once in a while. If it is warm, you are moving too fast. On the other hand, remember that fish does not have to be totally thawed before being cooked, unless it is going to be deep fried.

Cooking Partially or Completely Frozen Fish

A lot of our favorite recipes say to braise, bake, broil, and grill our steaks, fillets, and whole fish. All of these methods of cooking adapt well to the incompletely thawed fish. Completely frozen fish are best left to slower cooking methods like braising and baking under 400°F (205°C). For fish thawed on the outside, but frozen in the center, and less than 2 inches (5 cm) thick, allow one quarter to one third more cooking time, depending on how much of the fish is thawed. For completely frozen fish more than 2 inches (5 cm) thick, increase the cooking time by half.

Never deep-fry frozen fish; the water released from the tissue during cooking will spatter and burn the cook.

Testing for Doneness

The methods for testing whether or not a fish is done are legion, and the easiest way to describe doneness is to begin with a test. In any pan you wish, boil about 1 cup (250 ml) of water; then place a piece of fish, any fish, at least 1 inch square (2½ cm square) into the boiling water. What was once shiny and translucent—even transparent in some fish—turns white and opaque right before your eyes. If you remove the chunk of fish immediately after it turns opaque, it is done but moist; if you leave it boiling longer, it is done but getting dry. This is also a good way to determine how you want your fish to be finished. Some people like their fish slightly translucent—what is traditionally still raw (except in poached fish). Others like to take it past the moist-looking stage. Here are several traditional, time-honored

It helps to have everything chopped, grated, cleaned, and ready to start cooking, as fish always cooks up quickly.

Fly fishing Montana (Photo © Alan and Sandy Carey)

ways to test fish so that it is moist, but done.

1. Meat thermometer: Insert a meat thermometer into the thickest part of the fish, and remove the fish from the oven when the thermometer registers 125°F (52°C). The thermometer will rise 10°F (5°C) more in the first 10 minutes out of the oven; the final temperature should be 135°F (57°C).

2. Skin: The skin on a properly cooked fish will peel off easily, taking no flesh with it.

3. Texture: The oldest and most commonly used method to test fish is with a fork. Insert the fork into the thickest part of the fish, usually along the middle stretch of the spine, and gently twist. The flesh should give, not fall apart; and it should be moist-looking, rather than dry. While everyone talks about a fish being flaky, an over-cooked fish is also flaky, so look at both texture and shine.

4. Color: Pale- and white-fleshed fish like walleye and light trout will be opaque but shiny when ready. Orange-fleshed fish will be paler and less shiny than when raw. Look for the color of the fish when you flake it with a fork. When barbecuing, most whole fish will fan open when nearly done, and you can check the inside flesh, along the spine, for color. In fact, you can watch the flesh turn from translucent pink to opaque white, from the thin ribs to the thick back, as it cooks. Remove the fish as soon as the meat is white throughout, and you will have a moist fish.

Panfish are generally dredged in flour, cornmeal, or crumbled corn flakes, then fried whole with the skin on. If the fish are large enough, you can also fillet each side, skin, and cut the fillet into strips to be dredged in meal and fried. The trick, however, is not to overcook the tender flesh or let it absorb much of the oil.

Use peanut and canola oils, or any oil with an equally high smoking point, heat it to just below smoking, and fry the fish quickly, until each side is just golden, then remove it from the pan. If you are watching your fat intake, stick to peanut and canola oils, which are not only high-smoking, but are monounsaturated oils recommended by cardiologists. Or bake the fish at 400°F (205°C) until opaque, and flake the flesh off with your fingers to eat outright with a bit of cocktail sauce, or to add to a salad or other dish. When you are camping or there's no oven to use, simply poach the fish in a covered pan, in just enough water, white wine, or extra-dry vermouth to provide moist heat. Then flake as above.

THE CARE AND FEEDING OF KNIVES

I live 6 miles (9½ km) east of the Missouri River, and 6¼ miles (10 km) as the crow flies from one of the largest lakes in Montana—the first of three lakes on the mighty Missouri that not only hold the river, but walleye, perch, largemouth bass, Kokanee salmon, and luminous, fat rainbow trout as long as my Labrador's tail. With heaven out my front door, somehow it is the tiny creek—and equally tiny trout—out my back door that I fish spring, summer, and fall. It's a creek Kerri Strug could lay across and touch both banks, and needs only knee waders and a moderately perky woolly bugger to provide ample protein for supper.

That appeals to the frugal side in me—not having to buy, maintain, and insure a big boat, three motors, and a computer just to find an animal with a brain the size of a mosquito. It also appeals to the non-mechanical, dyslexic in me who can't sight in a bow without help and loves fishing with one dry fly, one Labrador, and a half-sharp, one-bladed Swiss army knife.

My little Kitchen Creek also appeals to the escapist in me: I prefer to cast my lure among the pines, not the *rat-a-tat-tat* of a single-cylinder engine—nor the *do wop* rumba of a big-lake boat. Unfortunately, the fish that appeal most to my taste buds are pretty hard to catch unless you have access to *rat-a-tat-tats* and *do wops*.

Oh, sure, I like brookies fried in cornmeal, cutbows spitted over an open fire creekside, and big browns smoked with a bit of jalapeño pepper. But, to bring home the pale-meated, flaky-textured, delicate-tasting freshwater fish that is not only America's favorite fish but mine, you need to negotiate deeper water than even $400 chest waders can accommodate. I am of course speaking not only of walleye, but also walleye's not too shabby-tasting fellow fish, pike and lunker largemouth and smallmouth bass. Fish large enough to make long, substantial fillets, steaks, and—with a little imagination—cook whole in the oven or barbecue and feed a crowd.

The thing is that whether you are fishing your own Kitchen Creek for one tiny trout, or the big water for a winter's worth of walleye, there is one piece of equipment you must stick in your pocket before venturing out: a knife. Long, short, carbide or stainless steel, a knife is eventually needed by everyone who ventures out to fish. If you are taking one little trout on a hot, lazy, summer's day, a dull knife will be frustrating, but do the job. Get more than one fish, or get a big fish, and you will be wishing that fancy electric knife sharpener you bought last Christmas had a longer extension cord. Your choice is to spend hundreds of dollars buying a covey of knives, sharpen them at home on an electric knife sharpener, and pray you never catch more fish than you have knives, or, more simple and less expensive to boot, buy a couple of rocks and learn the ancient and ageless method of sharpening one good knife anywhere you happen to be.

To Sharpen a Knife

Let's start with the ABC's. A) All knives are not sharpened the same way. B) A 30-degree angle isn't always a 30-degree angle. And, C) You don't have to take up transcendental meditation to carry a well-sharpened knife.

For equipment, you need a set of sharpening stones, 3–5 is sufficient, ranging from very coarse, to medium, to fine grain. Then you need something to fine tune the edge, or to quick hone an edge that is only slightly dull. A pair of ceramic crotch sticks, one diamond finishing stick or a steel will do the job. For those who really enjoy a sharp blade and have the time, a few passes with a leather strop will lay all the rough edges down for a truly smooth cutting edge.

Stones come in many shapes and sizes from pocket-sized to table-length, genuine Arkansas, imitation Arkansas, and even stones that claim no state affiliation at all. Diamond stones are not just for coarse work, either. They come in all grains, including a finishing grain as fine as any Arkansas stone. No matter what the stone or its content, the sharpening method is the same. The stone should be about the length of the knife, and absolutely flat—no nicks, gouges, or valleys. Whether you start with a very dull knife, or one that only needs

A variety of knife sharpeners

a little touch-up, the progression is the same, coarse to fine stones, then as much finishing work as you have time and temperament for. Now get out your old fillet knife, and let's put a good edge on it so it's ready for your next fishing trip.

To Sharpen a Moderately Dull Knife

The first thing you need to do is find the exact angle of the blade. Fillet knives are usually at a 28-degree bevel (meaning 14 degrees on one side, 14 degrees on the other), but often the factory sharpens the blade 1 to 3 degrees off that. Unless you want to rebuild the blade, you are best off following the factory's lead, using the bevels suggested above as a guide for finding the exact angle.

To find the exact angle, lay the knife flat on the left side of the sharpening stone with the blade pointed toward the right. Slowly and gently slide the blade across the stone, raising the angle of the blade as you go. At first, it will slide along with no resistance, then it will feel like the brakes are being applied. Remember that angle of the knife blade to the stone. That's the angle at which the knife was sharpened when it was made. Let's assume the angle you found was for a fillet knife at a 28-degree bevel. Now let's sharpen it. (Directions are for right-handed people.)

Using a moderately soft (coarse) stone, lay the

knife back on the left side of the sharpening stone, blade pointed to the right, and the hilt at the bottom edge. Tilt the blade at a 14-degree angle. If you are not sure what a 14-degree angle looks like or don't have a protractor, set the knife straight up at a 90-degree angle, then tip it halfway over—45 degrees. Fourteen is slightly less than a third of 45. Nothing mystical, just simple arithmetic. Now, with a steady hand, slide the blade once across the stone, being sure to maintain that 14-degree angle all the way. Imagine you are trying to slice off a thin, even layer of the stone. That's the principle: maintaining the angle, and sliding evenly. Any bumps, skips, or slips will mar the finished edge.

Like any good song, there's another chorus: While you slide across on the horizontal, move the knife vertically from hilt to tip so that the entire length of the blade—right out to the tip—is sharpened with one stroke. Flip the knife over, and lay the hilt on the right bottom edge of the stone and sharpen the second side as you did the first. After about four swipes, test the edge by placing it gently at a 45-degree angle to your finger nail. If you feel it grab, it's time to go to a fine stone or the ceramic sticks.

Use the fine stone as you did the softer stone. For the crotch sticks, place the knife at the same angle you used on the stone. Starting at the hilt—against the top of one stick, slide the knife down the stick again at a 14-degree angle, till the knife tip is at the bottom. Do the same with the other side of the blade, then alternately, five to seven times. Do the same with a steel flipping the blade with each stroke. Finally, for a perfect edge, do the same with the leather strop, except run the knife blade backwards—dragging the sharp edge behind—alternating one side of the blade then the other.

These last three tools fine tune the edge. When you sharpen a knife on a coarse stone you create miniature saw teeth which can break away or bend, dulling the knife. The harder (finer) stone and ceramic sticks make those teeth finer, which makes the edge hold longer. A steel aligns the teeth and smoothes them out; a strop adds another measure of smoothing and aligning. But you don't have to have a regulation strop, which are hard to find these days. An old leather belt, a cowboy boot, or even the leather sheath you carry your knife in, will do the job, too.

A sharp knife will cut a skinned, ripe orange without squashing it, while you can take a very dull knife and press your finger directly on the edge without getting cut. So, what if you have a really dull knife on your hands?

To Sharpen a Very Dull Knife

The important thing to remember is that the blade of a really dull knife is not shaped the same as a moderately dull knife. Instead of the blade being shaped like a V, it is shaped more like a U, bulged out above the blade edge. Before you start actually sharpening the edge, you need to shave off the bulge.

Lay the knife on the left end of the sharpening stone, blade pointed to the right, and hilt at the bottom edge of the stone. Slowly and gently slide the blade across the stone, raising the angle of the blade as you did before to find the exact angle. When you feel the brakes, stop. That is the U-bulge, not the real angle of the blade. Lower the blade slightly so that you don't feel the brakes and start sharpening at that angle. After ten to twelve swipes each side, do the fingernail test. If the edge drags, move on to a soft (coarse) Arkansas stone and continue sharpening as for the moderately dull knife.

Three more points: First, never sharpen even an extremely dull knife with a grinding wheel; the heat will change the temper of the blade, making the knife either brittle or soft, depending on how it cools. Second, you will find that with filleting knives more than hunting knives, the front end of

Getting lined out

the knife is used most and will dull faster. When you sharpen those fillet knives, always test that area especially to see if the whole knife is sharp no matter the condition of the knife when you start. And third, always sharpen the knife to the point that you are comfortable with. If you go through these steps once, and you still feel the knife is dull, run it through again. These directions are meant to work for you, not limit you.

Those extremely coarse diamond sharpening stones have become quite popular, and like many people, I have one tucked away in a kitchen drawer. But we keep our knives pretty sharp, so the soft Arkansas stone, while not as coarse as those diamonds, is usually the most radical stone we use. We keep one medium stone, a steel, and a pair of ceramic sticks in the kitchen, and John and I both carry a stone in our hunting pack. If you can't hold a steady angle or are just too tired after a hard day's fishing, the best cheater is a knife sharpening kit. These sets come with a variety of stones, from coarse to fine, and a contraption that you attach to the back of the knife blade that keeps the blade at the perfect angle while you work. We keep one of those kits in our kitchen too, for our guests, and the occasional knife that gets out of whack. If the knife is ruler dull, these sharpening kits make it a lot easier to keep the angle straight while you work at getting it back in shape.

And if nothing you do works, if you simply can't figure the angle, can't hold it straight, or don't have the time, inclination, or desire, buy yourself one of those precision magnetic angled sharpeners (from $90 to $400). Then do what I used to do before I learned how to use the stone: carry more than one knife, sharpen them before you leave home, and never fish with people who can't sharpen a knife.

To paraphrase an old friend: There's two things that ain't—good dull knives and a bad day of fishing.

Care and Maintenance of Sharpening Stones

There are two main theories on how to keep stones working over a long period of time. Some place a few drops of oil on the stone before sharpening, to prevent metal filings from clogging the pores and ruining the finish. I prefer sharpening dry, then cleaning the stone with a synthetic scrub sponge and hot soapy water to remove filings.

Caring for Ceramic Sharpening Sticks

According to my friends in the sport-catalog business, ceramic sticks aren't popular anymore because they get coated with metal filings and quit working too quickly. My ceramic sticks are over twenty years old and still work. The secret is to clean them periodically with a synthetic scrubber sponge and some soft, liquid scouring powder. Having said that, I admit that my brand new diamond steel is faster. But isn't all brand new stuff always faster?

Choosing a Good Fillet Knife

Try this experiment: Place your fillet knife tip-down on a cutting board and apply just enough pressure to get it to bend easily. Some fillet knives will bend slightly, others bow out quite wide. I prefer the stouter blade, the one that doesn't bow out, since the strength of the blade prevents it from bending and twisting when I am filleting any fish large enough to get a decent fillet. It also gives you a neater fillet, without gouges and false starts. Save the more flexible blade for very small fish, or for trimming off flesh that doesn't come with the big fillet, to use for soups and fish cakes.

The good news is that fillet knives are relatively cheap. They can be made out of fairly thin sheet metal and don't have to be milled since they are not thick blades.

Metal Properties

Knife blades are made of steel, either carbide or stainless. For years it was believed that only carbide could be sharpened easily, but in the last decade, stainless knives have been perfected to the point that they are just as easy to sharpen and also maintain an edge. Around water, it's hard to beat a stainless knife with a plastic handle.

COOL-WATER AND
WARM-WATER FISH

WALLEYE

WALLEYE SHORE DINNER

Yield: 1 dinner (or lunch) for a boatful, usually 4 servings

Walleye fishing almost always involves a boat, and if you've got a boat, you can carry a few things to make life just a bit more luxurious than if you were wading up a tiny trout stream. Luxuries may include things like rain gear and pop, but they should always include a frying pan (or two) and a little bacon to grease it—all the better to enjoy a truly fresh walleye fillet. The culinary principle here is: If you can catch a fish—and steer a boat to shore—you won't starve.

Ingredients

8 ounces (200 g) bacon
6 potatoes, sliced ¼ inch (½ cm) thick
1 onion, sliced
1 teaspoon salt
1 teaspoon pepper
1 cup (250 ml) cornmeal
2 pounds (1 kg) walleye fillets

Cooking

1. Warm two 8-inch (20-cm) frying pans over medium heat, and divide the bacon between the two. Cook the bacon until crisp, then remove it from the pans. In one pan, combine the potatoes and onion, season with half the salt and pepper, and cook until the potatoes are tender, about 20–30 minutes.

2. While the potatoes and onions cook, remove the second pan from the fire, and prepare the fish. In a shallow bowl, combine the cornmeal with the rest of the salt and pepper, and dredge the fillets in this mixture. No need to dry the fillets; the cornmeal will soak up the moisture and prevent the fat from spattering.

3. When the potatoes are about done, heat the second pan on high until the fat is hot, and gently place the walleye fillets in the hot fat. Cook until golden brown on both sides, about 7–8 minutes. Serve your shore dinner with that all-American vegetable—ketchup.

WALLEYE RAREBIT ON GARLIC TOAST

Yield: 6 servings

Glance down at the directions in this recipe and you'll notice the rarebit is cooked in a double boiler. Now I don't own a double boiler, so I use what a lot of people have used for years: a metal bowl set in a pot of boiling water. The double-pot system allows the cheese to melt gently without fear of burning, while being able to apply a great deal of heat. (I've tried making rarebit in the microwave, but there's no way to "stir continuously" in that quick, but not entirely perfect, appliance. Thus, the rarebit fails.) In fact, this sauce goes together faster than the fish cooks—so it helps to have all the ingredients ready to go before you start cooking this quick and delicious lunch.

Previous page: *Walleye (Photo © Doug Stamm/ProPhoto)*

Ingredients

1 loaf Italian or French bread

2 teaspoons cooking oil

1 clove garlic, minced

2 pounds (1 kg) walleye fillets, 1 inch (2½ cm) thick

1 tablespoon butter or margarine

⅔ cup (160 ml) lager or pale ale beer

¼ teaspoon dry mustard

Dash of cayenne pepper

8 ounces (200 g) Cheddar cheese, grated

1 egg, lightly beaten

Cooking

1. Preheat broiler for 10 minutes. Fill a double boiler with about 2 inches (5 cm) of water, and bring to a boil. Cut the bread in 1½-inch-thick (4-cm) slices. In a small bowl, combine the oil and garlic, and brush it on one side of the bread. Rinse and pat dry the fillets, and cut into individual portions the same size as the toast.

2. Lightly oil your broiler pan and place the fillets on it. Place the broiler pan in the center of the oven, about 4–5 inches (10–13 cm) from the flame and cook the fish for 8–10 minutes, or until it is flaky but looks moist.

3. As soon as you start the fish, start the rarebit sauce. Melt the butter in the double boiler, and stir in the beer, mustard, and cayenne pepper. When the beer is warm to the touch, add the cheese. Stir constantly as the cheese melts, keeping the water under the rarebit sauce at a low boil. Finally, when the cheese is melted, add the beaten egg, and stir to mix thoroughly. The rarebit takes about 5 minutes total.

4. By now the fish should be about three-quarters done. Place the bread, garlic side up on the broiler rack, and broil about 3 minutes until it is browned. When the fish is flaky but moist, remove the toast and fish fillets, and assemble your walleye rarebit: Place the fillet on the garlic toast and spoon a generous portion of rarebit over the top. If you want, brown the rarebit under the broiler. Serve with French-cut green beans.

FISH CAKES BALTIMORE

Yield: 6 servings

You don't need to use walleye to make these fish cakes, but fish cakes are one of those forgiving dishes that allows you to use all the tasty tidbits left on the bone and the thin strips you trim off fillets. Keep a freezer bag for these small bites of fish and don't be afraid to mix pike or bass in with the walleye. Any pale-fleshed fish will do.

Ingredients

¼ cup (60 ml) margarine
1 medium onion, chopped
¼ cup (60 ml) minced parsley
½ cup (125 ml) flour
1 cup (250 ml) milk
4 eggs
1 ½ pounds (¾ kg) fish, finely chopped
¼ teaspoon salt
¼ teaspoon pepper
1 cup (250 ml) cracker crumbs
¼ cup (60 ml) cooking oil

Cooking

1. In a large skillet, melt the margarine over medium heat. Sauté the onion and parsley until the onion is tender, about 5 minutes. Add the flour and stir until the vegetables are well coated. Combine the milk and two of the eggs in a separate bowl, and stir them into the onion mixture. Cook until the egg and milk thicken and start to pull away from the sides of the pan. Remove from the heat. Fold in the fish chunks, season with salt and pepper, and set the mixture aside to cool.

2. Place the cracker crumbs in one bowl and lightly beat the last two eggs in a second shallow bowl. Form the fish mixture into patties 2–3 inches (5–7 ½ cm) in diameter (the smaller for appetizers, the larger for dinner) and about ½ inch (1 ¼ cm) thick. Dip the patties into the egg, then into the crackers.

3. Heat the oil in the skillet over medium heat and cook the patties until they are golden brown, about 2 minutes per side. Drain the fish cakes on a paper towel and serve hot, with scalloped potatoes.

ON PARSLEY

Often used in fish recipes, and always much better fresh, parsley is highly perishable and hard to come by in most small-town grocery stores. I live in such a small town and have learned that parsley will last a lot longer if you treat it as you would cut flowers. Lay your bunch of parsley on a cutting board, cut ½ inch (1 ¼ cm) off the stems, then place them upright in cold, clean water. Do this as soon as you bring it home, and again every three to four days, and your parsley will last two weeks. And if you don't think a bunch of rabbit food is worth all this trouble, rub a bit of dried parsley flakes in your hand. Now cut the fresh with a pair of scissors. The difference in taste is like store tomatoes versus home grown.

And if you're not tired of parsley trivia yet, the easiest way to mince the unruly stuff is with a scissors. Start by clipping about twice as many leaves from the stem as you think you'll need into a measuring cup. Then turn the scissors point down inside the cup, and clip away until the parsley is "minced."

WALLEYE FILLETS BAKED IN PARCHMENT

Yield: 4 servings

Technically this is *en papillote*, a French term meaning food cooked and served in a greased paper bag—or now, aluminum foil. So if you have ever stuck an animal in foil and sealed it up to cook, you are using this classic method. Starting with the paper or aluminum envelope, the variations are endless, from a simple squeeze of lemon to a fillet sitting on a *mirepoix*—sautéed aromatic vegetables. The method is quite versatile, perfect for those who want to limit their fat intake as well as those who simply want a delicately moist fillet at the table.

Fly fishing in western Montana (Photo © Alan and Sandy Carey)

Ingredients

1 teaspoon salt
1 teaspoon pepper
1 teaspoon dried thyme leaf
$\frac{1}{2}$ teaspoon fennel seeds
1 bay leaf
4 tablespoons heavy cream
2 pounds (1 kg) walleye fillets, 1 inch (2$\frac{1}{2}$ cm) thick
Orange peel, grated

Cooking

1. Preheat oven to 500°F (255°C). In a food processor or blender, combine the salt, pepper, thyme, fennel seeds, bay leaf, and cream. Purée until the fennel seeds and bay leaf are coarsely chopped.
2. Rinse and pat dry the fillets. Trim them, and divide into four portions. Cut baking parchment (or aluminum foil) into four rectangles large enough to wrap each of the portions. Lightly brush each rectangle with oil, then spread 1 tablespoon of the seasoned cream mixture in the center of each. Place the walleye on the cream, sprinkle with a dash of the orange peel, and close up the packet, folding the edges together.
3. Place the packets slightly apart on a lightly oiled baking sheet. Bake about 7–10 minutes, checking the fillets for doneness by cutting a tiny slit through the parchment. The fish is done when the walleye flakes easily, is slightly translucent or wet inside, and is opaque.
4. Place each packet on a plate. To serve, cut open the packets just enough to get at the fish without losing the juices. Serve with fettucini tossed with olive oil and Parmesan cheese.

CRACKER MEAL FILLETS WITH SEASONED OVEN FRIES

Yield: 4 servings

The only thing easier than crunching crackers is snagging a ten-dollar lure in twenty feet of water. So use a prepackaged cracker meal, or crunch your favorite cracker, from Cheese-Its to Ritz to Wheat Thins, and adapt this oldest of recipes to your own changing (or never-have-changed-since-the-fifties) taste buds.

Cracker Meal Fillets with Seasoned Oven Fries

Ingredients

2 pounds (1 kg) walleye fillets, 1 inch (2 ½ cm) thick
2 eggs
2 tablespoons lemon juice
2 cups (500 ml) cracker meal
1 teaspoon nutmeg

4 medium red potatoes
2 tablespoons cooking oil
1 teaspoon salt
1 teaspoon pepper
1 teaspoon garlic powder
3 tablespoons Parmesan cheese
1 tablespoon butter

Classic bait store on Alaska's Kenai Peninsula (Photo © Alissa Crandall)

Cooking

1. Rinse and pat dry the walleye fillets and cut into individual serving size. Crack the eggs into a shallow bowl, add the lemon juice, and beat lightly with a fork. Put the cracker meal and nutmeg in a second shallow bowl and stir to combine.

2. Preheat the broiler for 10 minutes. Slice the potatoes $\frac{1}{4}$ inch ($\frac{1}{2}$ cm) thick, then stack the slices and cut them into $\frac{1}{4}$-inch ($\frac{1}{2}$-cm) strips, so you have evenly cut fries. Place the fries into a plastic bag or covered dish, and add 1 tablespoon of the oil, and all the salt, pepper, garlic powder, and Parmesan cheese. Toss gently to coat. Lay these fries out in a single layer on two cookie sheets. Place about 4 inches (10 cm) under the broiler and cook about 7 minutes; flip the fries with a spatula and give the other side about 4–6 minutes until the potatoes are golden brown and the cheese is starting to bubble. When both sheets are done, turn the broiler off, and place the potatoes on a lower oven shelf to keep warm.

3. While the potatoes cook, start the fillets: In a large skillet, melt the butter over medium-high heat, then add the second tablespoon of oil. You should have about $\frac{1}{4}$ inch ($\frac{1}{2}$ cm) of fat in the pan; if you don't, add equal amounts of oil and butter until you do.

4. When the fat is hot but not smoking, quickly dip the fillets in the egg then in the cracker meal and gently place them in the pan. Cook until golden brown on both sides, about 4–5 minutes a side or 8–10 minutes total for each 1 inch ($2\frac{1}{2}$ cm) of thickness. Do not overcook: Even butter-fried fish needs to stay moist looking, while flaky. Serve both the cracker meal fillets and the oven fries piping hot.

Note: For cooking oil, I prefer peanut or canola oil as they both have a high smoking point. The combination of half butter and half high-smoking point oil gives you both flavor and quick cooking—without burning.

SATURDAY CROQUETTES

Yield: 4 servings, or about 10 croquettes

Leftover walleye and leftover mashed potatoes never tasted so good. Make the croquettes big for a main course, as shown here, or golf ball–sized for appetizers. They're crunchy on the outside and, if you substitute 1 sweet potato in your mashings, they'll be extra rich inside.

Above: *For an endless—and inexpensive—supply of bread crumbs, bake any type of bread in a single layer in your oven for 30 minutes at 200°F (90°C). Cool 10 minutes, and crumble by hand or in a food processor.*

Right: *Saturday Croquettes*

Ingredients

2 cups (500 ml) cold mashed potatoes
2 eggs
2 teaspoons dried parsley flakes
2 tablespoons chopped green onion
$\frac{1}{2}$ teaspoon salt
$\frac{1}{2}$ teaspoon pepper
1 tablespoon grated Parmesan cheese
8 ounces (200 g) cooked and flaked walleye
1 tablespoon water
1 cup (250 ml) fine bread crumbs
Peanut or canola oil for frying

Cooking

1. Combine the mashed potatoes with one of the eggs, the parsley, green onion, salt, pepper, and Parmesan cheese. Gently fold in the flaked walleye. Shape into approximately 10 balls, about 2 inches (5 cm) in diameter. In a separate bowl, combine the other egg with the water. Put the bread crumbs in another shallow bowl. Roll the croquettes in the bread crumbs, then in the egg-water mixture, and then in the bread crumbs again. Set on a sheet of waxed paper and let stand at least 15 minutes, turning occasionally, to allow the coating to set.

2. Fill the deep-fat fryer with peanut or canola oil to manufacturer's suggested level, then preheat to 375°F (190°C). Deep-fry the croquettes two or three at a time until dark golden brown and crisp, about 3 minutes. Drain on a paper towel. Serve with cole slaw and garlic bread.

Note: Most deep-fat fryers operate at 375°F (190°C) even though they don't have a built-in thermometer. You can use a candy thermometer if you do not trust your fryer to reach 375°F (190°C) in 10 minutes.

OVEN-BROILED WALLEYE FILLETS WITH *BUERRE BLANC*

Yield: 4 servings

The French have a way of saying things that make your mouth water. Take *buerre blanc*. The *buerre* is butter, the *blanc* white wine. If you can't get a dry white wine to make the sauce right, you can substitute extra-dry vermouth or even an inexpensive bottle of extra-dry (*brut*, in French) champagne. Perhaps a better name for this dish is *Brut Buerre Blanc*, but I'd have a hard time saying it six times fast. For the garlic lovers in the family, add two cloves of minced garlic when you sauté the onion.

Ingredients

2 pounds (1 kg) walleye fillets
2 green onions, minced
$\frac{1}{4}$ cup (60 ml) dry white wine
$\frac{1}{4}$ cup (60 ml) white wine vinegar
6 tablespoons butter
$\frac{1}{2}$ teaspoon salt
$\frac{1}{4}$ teaspoon pepper

Cooking

1. Cut the fillets into serving-sized pieces and pat dry. Preheat the broiler and broiler pan for 10 minutes. In a small saucepan, combine the onions, white wine, and vinegar. Bring to a low simmer and cook until the liquid is reduced to about 2 tablespoons. Keep an eye on it, but you only need to give it an occasional stir.

2. Remove the broiler pan from the oven, and spray or brush lightly with oil. Do the same with the fillets. Place the fillets on the broiler pan, about 4 inches (10 cm) from the fire. Check in about 6 minutes to see how they're doing; but they should take 8–10 minutes. The fish is done when you insert a fork at the thickest part, twist, and the fish flakes but is still moist looking.

3. While the fillets are cooking, finish the sauce: To the reduced wine mixture, add the butter, 1 tablespoon at a time, as you stir or whisk vigorously over low heat. The butter will both bind and thicken your sauce. Season with salt and pepper. Serve immediately over your broiled fillets with fresh artichokes on the side.

Lemony Stuffed Walleye Rolls

Yield: 4 servings

If you don't have as much time as you'd like, streamline the recipe by just rolling the fish fillets naked—without the stuffing—and then make the lemon sauce. It's almost as elegant but takes half the time.

Lemony Stuffed Walleye Rolls ready to cook

Ingredients

1 cup (250 ml) minced onion
½ cup (125 ml) minced celery
1 carrot, minced
1 tablespoon cooking oil
4 cups (1 liter) dried bread cubes
2 tablespoons diced, fresh parsley
1 cup (250 ml) fish broth or dry white wine

1 teaspoon salt
1 teaspoon pepper
4 walleye fillets, about 2 pounds (1 kg)
½ cup (125 ml) freshly squeezed lemon juice, about 3 small or 2 large lemons
4 tablespoons dry vermouth or white wine
1 tablespoon sour cream
Pinch of cayenne pepper

Cooking

1. In a large skillet over medium heat, sauté the onion, celery, and carrot in the oil until tender and slightly golden. Add the bread cubes and parsley, and toss to coat. When the vegetables and bread are nicely mixed, stir in 1 cup (250 ml) of fish broth or white wine to moisten the stuffing mix. Season with the salt and pepper. Remove from heat and set aside.

2. Preheat oven to 350°F (175°C). Rinse and pat dry the walleye fillets. Lay them out on the counter or cutting board, and with the palm of your hand, gently press the fillets to about ¼-inch (½-cm) thickness, being careful not to tear them. (That's why you do it with your hand rather than a rolling pin, so you can feel if the flesh begins to tear.) Once the fillets are relatively flat, cover them with the stuff-ing mix. Press this gently into the flesh to make it stick while you roll up the fillets. Lay the rolled fillets seam side down in a lightly oiled baking dish. Spread any remaining stuffing among the rolls, and pour the lemon juice and vermouth over all.

3. Bake, uncovered, for 30 minutes. When done, the fish will be white and moist look-ing. Carefully remove the rolled fillets to a heated platter, and place the baking dish on a burner at medium heat. Stir in the sour cream and continue cooking until the pan juices thicken up, 2–4 minutes. Mash any errant bread cubes into the sauce. Spoon the sauce over the rolled fillets and garnish with a pinch of cayenne pepper. Serve with fresh garden peas.

Piping hot Lemony Stuffed Walleye Rolls ready to eat

WALLEYE FILLETS FLORENTINE

Yield: 4 servings

Walleye is perfect for this classic French baked dish because the flesh is pale and delicate tasting, but while that makes the fish good to eat, it is much more likely than pike to fall apart in the pan. Since this Florentine is baked in the oven, and the fish isn't folded, spindled, or mutilated in cooking, our favorite eating fish is in no danger. This cream sauce also transforms fish into the most creamy-textured edible you can imagine.

Walleye Fillets Florentine

Ingredients

1 bunch fresh spinach, about 1 pound ($\frac{1}{2}$ kg)
$\frac{1}{2}$ teaspoon salt
$\frac{1}{2}$ teaspoon white pepper
1$\frac{1}{2}$ pounds ($\frac{3}{4}$ kg) walleye fillets, 1 inch
    (2$\frac{1}{2}$ cm) thick
2 tablespoons butter
2 tablespoons flour
$\frac{3}{4}$ cup (185 ml) half and half
$\frac{1}{4}$ cup (60 ml) extra-dry vermouth, or dry
    white wine
2 ounces (50 g) Swiss cheese, grated

Cooking

1. Wash the spinach leaves carefully in cold water; leave wet. In a large skillet over medium heat, cook the wet spinach leaves until just limp. (This process is called "sweating" the spinach, if you want to be indelicate.) Now squeeze out the excess moisture in a colander or with your hands, and mince. Toss with $\frac{1}{4}$ teaspoon of the salt and $\frac{1}{4}$ teaspoon of the pepper, and arrange in the bottom of a buttered 9x13-inch (22x32-cm) baking dish.

2. Rinse and pat dry the walleye fillets. Place on top of the spinach, tucking in and overlapping thin fillet ends to keep a uniform cooking thickness.

3. Preheat oven to 375°F (190°C). In a saucepan, melt the butter over medium heat, stir in the flour until all the liquid has been absorbed, and gradually add the half and half, stirring constantly. The sauce will be thick at first, then thin out. Continue cooking until it thickens up again, to the consistency of good turkey gravy, about 10 minutes. Stir in the vermouth and cheese, season with the rest of the salt and pepper, and continue cooking until the cheese is melted and the sauce smooth again. Spoon over the fish fillets and spinach.

4. Bake, uncovered, for 15 minutes, or until the thickest part of the fillet flakes easily but is still shiny and moist looking. Place under the broiler to brown, 2–3 minutes. Serve with fresh spring asparagus.

Note: You can make this traditional white sauce more quickly in the microwave: Combine the half and half, vermouth, and flour in a 1-quart (1-liter) microwaveable bowl and stir well. Add the butter and microwave for 2 minutes at 500 watts (about 1 minute 20 seconds at 700 watts). Remove from the microwave, and give the sauce a good stir. Microwave about 2–3 more minutes, stirring it down every 30 seconds, until the sauce bubbles up and thickens. Stir in the grated cheese.

Oven-Poached Walleye

Yield: 4 servings

I know of only one way to make this recipe any easier than it is already, and that is to buy too much rosemary-, thyme-, and sage-seasoned bread cubes at Thanksgiving and Christmas. Then instead of mixing a few spices, all you need to do is crunch the cubes. But it really is easy to make your own flavored bread crumbs, and when you make your own, the variations are infinite. You'll notice there's no added fat in this recipe: The little bit of vermouth in the baking pan and the light coating of bread crumbs are enough to keep the fish quite moist.

Ingredients
8 slices white bread, dried
1 teaspoon dried rosemary
½ teaspoon dried thyme leaf
½ teaspoon dried summer savory
2 teaspoons dried parsley flakes
1 teaspoon salt
½ teaspoon pepper
2 pounds (1 kg) walleye fillets, 1 inch (2½ cm) thick
½ cup (125 ml) extra-dry vermouth

Cooking
1. Preheat oven to 400°F (205°C). Cube the dry bread and place in a food processor. Process until crumbly, then add the rosemary, thyme, savory, parsley, salt, and pepper, and process 3–5 seconds more. Pour this mixture into a shallow bowl.

2. Rinse the fillets and drip dry. Then dredge in the bread crumb mixture and place in a buttered baking dish, in a single layer. Carefully pour the vermouth around the fillets until it is about ¼ inch (½ cm) deep, then spread the last of the bread crumbs over the fillets.

3. Bake in the middle of the oven, about 20 minutes, uncovered. The fish is done when you insert a fork at the thickest part, twist, and the fish flakes but is still moist looking. Serve with fresh garden green beans and a white wine risotto.

WALLEYE FRITTERS CARIBBEAN STYLE

Yield: 6 servings

When you're all done filleting your catch, there's still a good bit of meat on the bones you don't want to waste. But what can you do with those little chunks? Gumbo, chowder, fish balls, fish cakes. But if you have a hunger for hot stuff, you owe it to yourself to try this Caribbean twist: the scotch bonnet chili. Scotch bonnet may not sound like much, but it packs a wallop that is more cumulative than immediate. (A word to the wise?) If you can't find these Caribbean chilies, try habanero, or another hi-octane variety. And use rubber gloves when you handle them—dried or fresh. The active ingredients stay active on your fingers for several days.

Walleye Fritters Caribbean Style

Ingredients

½ pound (¼ kg) walleye chunks
¼ cup (60 ml) chopped green onions
¼ cup (60 ml) chopped fresh parsley
1 teaspoon dried thyme leaf
3 cloves garlic, minced
1 scotch bonnet, or habanero chili, seeded and minced

1 cup (250 ml) milk
1⅓ cups (330 ml) flour
1 egg, lightly beaten
Peanut or canola oil for frying
1 teaspoon salt
1 lime, cut in wedges

Cooking

1. In a large bowl, combine the walleye with the green onions, parsley, thyme, garlic, and chili and mix well. In a separate bowl, combine the milk, flour, and egg and stir until just smooth. Gently stir the milk mixture into the fish mixture.

2. Fill the deep-fat fryer with peanut or canola oil to manufacturer's suggested level, then preheat to 375°F (190°C). When the oil is hot, test it by dropping 1 tablespoon of the batter into the oil. The fritter should be deep brown in 3–4 minutes. After your test, you can cook several tablespoon-sized fritters at the same time—just be sure they float freely and are not crowded together. Remove the fritters from the fryer and sprinkle lightly with salt as they drain on a paper towel. Serve hot, with a squeeze of lime.

Note: If all you can find is dry chili, let it soak 15–20 minutes in a bit of the milk to soften, then purée in a blender. If using fresh chili, it is the seeds and white, inner ribbing they cling to that hold a lot of the heat. If you are not into hot stuff, be sure to remove both before cooking—using rubber gloves to handle all hot peppers. Heat seekers are on their own.

BEER BATTER FILLETS WITH COCKTAIL SAUCE

Yield: 4 servings

If you don't have a beer to waste—or don't want to—you can substitute club soda. But use something bubbly, and make sure your fat is hot. Most single-temperature deep-fat fryers operate at 375°F (190°C), as recommended in this recipe, and that keeps the fish, and the batter, from absorbing much fat. Peanut and canola oil both have a high smoking point, which means they will last longer in your fryer, but they are both also monounsaturated—canola apparently being the more olive oil–like of the two and thus, healthier for us all.

Cocktail Sauce Ingredients

½ cup (125 ml) canned tomato purée
2 tablespoons cream-style prepared horse-radish
1 teaspoon fresh lemon juice

Fish Batter Ingredients

1 cup (250 ml) flour
¼ cup (60 ml) cornmeal
1 egg, lightly beaten
¼ teaspoon paprika
¼ teaspoon salt
⅛ teaspoon pepper
½ cup (125 ml) lager beer
Peanut oil for frying
1 pound (½ kg) walleye fillets

Preparation

1. To make the cocktail sauce: Combine the tomato purée, horseradish, and lemon juice in a small bowl, cover, and refrigerate 1–4 hours.

2. To make the fish batter: In a large bowl, combine the flour, cornmeal, egg, paprika, salt, pepper, and beer, and mix well. Let sit for 1 hour at room temperature.

Cooking

Fill the deep-fat fryer with peanut oil to manufacturer's suggested level, then preheat to 375°F (190°C). When the fryer is ready, pat dry, then dip each walleye fillet into the batter, and fry about 3 minutes until the batter is golden brown and the fish is flaky inside. Drain on a paper towel, then serve hot with the cocktail sauce and macaroni and cheese.

BARBECUED WALLEYE STEAKS WITH LEMON BUTTER

Yield: 4 servings

If you grill fish, you have already discovered the ancient flip debate: Turn a fillet or steak with a spatula and you need a doctorate in chefology to keep the flesh together. Cook it skin on, omit the flip, and you end up with grill marks on only one side. And, what else do you grill for, except the beauty of the grid? For once, a compromise is not a compromise: Grate it—hinged grate, that is—and have the best of both schools.

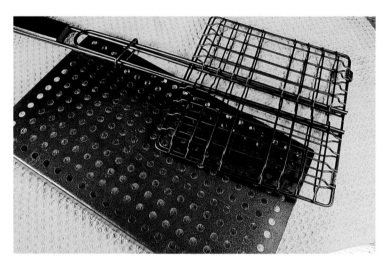

Cooking

1. To prepare the steaks: Preheat a propane barbecue on high for 10 minutes, then turn down to medium high. Or start four dozen charcoal briquettes and wait 25 minutes. The fire, on either grill, is ready when you can hold your hand at cooking level for just 4–5 seconds. To adjust the charcoal fire, spread the coals to lower the heat; pile them up to raise it. If you are using a hinged grate to hold the fish, preheat the grate for 10 minutes, too.

2. In a small bowl, melt the 2 tablespoons of butter in the microwave, and combine with the Worcestershire sauce.

3. Dry the steaks with a paper towel, then lightly brush the grilling surface or hinged grate (while it is away from the fire) with cooking oil; this will help prevent sticking. Grill the steaks about 3–4 minutes to a side, brushing with the Worcestershire and butter mixture several times. The fish is done when you insert a fork at the thickest part, twist, and the fish flakes but is still moist looking. Serve with a slice of lemon butter.

Note: Most of us are used to salmon and pike steaks, but there's no reason not to take steaks from a walleye as well. Larger fish are best, though, because you want a steak to be at least 3–4 inches (7½–10 cm) across and 1–1½ inches (2½–4 cm) thick.

The hinged barbecue grate is a good way to keep fish from falling apart on the grill.

Lemon Butter Ingredients

¼ pound (100 g) butter
1 teaspoon grated lemon peel
2 tablespoons minced green onions
Salt and pepper, to taste

Steaks Ingredients

2 tablespoons butter
1 tablespoon Worcestershire sauce
2 pounds (1 kg) walleye steaks, 1 inch (2½ cm) thick

Preparation

To prepare the lemon butter: In a small bowl, melt the ¼ pound (100 g) of butter in a microwave until it is soft but not liquid. Add the lemon peel and green onions, then season to taste with salt and pepper. Shape into a roll on a piece of waxed paper and chill 2–4 hours. Slice into patties when you are ready to serve.

WALLEYE NEWBURG

Yield: 6 servings

Newburg is one of my favorite ways to prepare fish. It is rich in both flavor and texture and is an elegant addition to holiday meals or any special occasion. And while it is traditionally made with a medley of shellfish, there is no reason a delicious fish like walleye should not be included in this company.

Ingredients

1 pound ($\frac{1}{2}$ kg) walleye fillets
4 ounces (112 g) shrimp, shelled and cleaned
4 ounces (112 g) lobster or crab meat
1 cup (250 ml) butter
2 cups (500 ml) heavy cream
$\frac{1}{2}$ teaspoon salt
Dash of cayenne pepper
$\frac{1}{8}$ teaspoon nutmeg
2 egg yolks
$\frac{1}{4}$ cup (60 ml) dry sherry
12 slices of toast, crust removed

Cooking

1. Rinse the fish in cold water, then pat dry with a paper towel.

2. To make toast cups: Preheat oven to 400°F (205°C). Butter the insides of a standard-sized muffin tin. Cut the crusts off each slice of bread, then trim to a $3\frac{1}{2}$ x $3\frac{1}{2}$-inch (9x9-cm) square. Gently tuck each square into a muffin cup to line the bottom and sides. Bake in the oven until the edges begin to brown, about 10 minutes. Let cool on a rack while you prepare the sauce.

3. Melt the butter in a large skillet. Sauté the mixed shellfish and walleye in the butter until the shrimp turns pink and the walleye opaque. Add all but 2 tablespoons of the cream, and continue to cook on medium heat until the mixture begins to boil. Reduce the heat and add the salt, cayenne, and nutmeg. Beat the egg yolks into the remaining 2 tablespoons of cream and stir into the skillet. Stir constantly until the sauce thickens, without boiling, then add the sherry and continue cooking until the sherry is heated through. Serve in the toast cups for a fancy occasion, or simply serve on toast or over rice.

Note: While predicting the weight of walleye is easy, the shellfish offer more of a challenge. To get 4 ounces (112 g) of shrimp, buy $\frac{1}{2}$ pound (200 g) of shrimp headless, raw. For 4 ounces (112 g) lobster or hardshell crab meat, buy 1 to $1\frac{1}{2}$ pound (450 to 750 g) in the shell. Mix and match as your pocketbook allows, for a total of 8 ounces (200 g).

WALLEYE VERACRUZ

Yield: 4 servings

Braised in a sauce of fresh tomatoes, capers, and chopped olives, this is a light, but quite tasty fish dish. It also cooks up fairly quickly, and is suitable for a Coleman stove or campfire meal.

Ingredients

⅓ cup (80 ml) cooking oil
3 medium potatoes, diced
1 onion, chopped
3 cloves garlic, minced
1 can chopped tomatoes, 28 ounces (795 g)
10 green olives, pitted and sliced
1 tablespoon capers, drained
2 bay leaves
1 teaspoon dried leaf cilantro
½ teaspoon dried leaf oregano
1 teaspoon salt
½ teaspoon pepper
2 pounds (1 kg) walleye fillets

Cooking

1. In a large skillet, heat the oil over medium-high heat, then lightly brown the diced potatoes, about 5 minutes. Remove the potatoes from the pan with a slotted spoon and set aside. Turn the skillet down to medium heat, and sauté the onion and garlic until tender but not browned. Return the browned potatoes to the skillet and stir in the tomatoes, olives, capers, bay leaves, cilantro, oregano, salt, and pepper. Bring to a gentle simmer. Simmer about 10 minutes, until the potatoes are fork tender but not mushy. Meanwhile, dry the fillets with a paper towel.

2. When the potatoes are tender, gently submerge the fillets in the vegetable mixture and cover, cooking about 5 minutes more or until the fish turns opaque and flakes easily. Remove the bay leaves. Carefully transfer the fillets to each plate, arrange the potatoes around them and spoon the sauce over the top.

Walleye Veracruz

CIOPPINO

Yield: 4 servings

One of the wonderful things about walleye—and pike—is that you can add it to any stew or soup and it will take on the other flavors. *Cioppino* is the perfect vehicle for such a blending. Traditionally made with lots of crab, since it was Portuguese and Italian crabbers plying their trade in the waters around San Francisco who invented it, *cioppino* is a stew that takes to any waters. Use big chunks of walleye, or use the firmer pike if you wish.

Ingredients

6 ounces (168 g) shrimp with shell on
12 ounces (336 g) crab legs with shell on
3 ounces (84 g) scallops
1 onion, coarsely chopped
1 clove garlic, minced
1 stalk celery, chopped, with leaves
1 tablespoon cooking oil
1 bay leaf
$\frac{1}{2}$ teaspoon dried leaf oregano
$\frac{1}{4}$ teaspoon ground sage
$\frac{1}{2}$ teaspoon salt
$\frac{1}{4}$ teaspoon pepper
1 can whole peeled tomatoes, 28 ounces
    (784 g)
8 ounces (200 g) walleye fillet or chunks

Cioppino

Preparation

Shell the crab legs and shrimp, saving the shells in a small saucepan. Cover the shellfish meats and refrigerate. Cover the shells with cold water, then bring to a boil over high heat. Lower the heat to a simmer, and let the shell broth cook down on the back burner while you prepare the rest of the *cioppino*.

Cooking

1. In a large, heavy-bottomed soup pot or kettle, sauté the onion, garlic, and celery in the oil over medium heat until tender. Add the bay leaf, oregano, sage, salt, and pepper and stir into the vegetables. Let cook another 3–4 minutes. Add the tomatoes with their liquid and simmer covered about 45 minutes. Half-way through this cooking time, strain $\frac{1}{2}$ cup (125 ml) of liquid off the shell broth and add it to the pot. (Let the rest of the shell broth continue cooking, until the *cioppino* is done, then cool and freeze for later soups, or use for poaching liquid.)

2. Cut the shellfish and walleye into bite-sized portions and stir gently into the simmering *cioppino*. Cook about 3–4 minutes more, until the walleye is opaque—do not overcook. Serve immediately with oyster crackers or toast.

Note: When purchasing shellfish, double the weight of meat needed to determine how much unshelled shrimp to buy, and quadruple it for crab legs. So, for 3 ounces (84 g) of shrimp meat, buy 6 ounces (168 g) raw in the shell. The money spent on shells will ad in richness of flavor when you make shell broth.

OVEN-BRAISED WHOLE WALLEYE IN RED WINE AND CREAM SAUCE

Yield: 4 servings

If you're going to break the biggest rule in fish cookery—namely that fish should only be served with white wine—I think you'd better do it in style. And don't let the word "style" put you off. If you can stir fry vegetables and make gravy, you can make this dish.

Oven-Braised Whole Walleye in Red Wine and Cream Sauce

Ingredients

1 whole walleye, 2 pounds (1 kg)
½ teaspoon salt
¼ teaspoon pepper
5 tablespoons butter
2 carrots, thinly sliced
3 stalks celery, chopped
1 large onion, chopped
½ pound (200 g) mushrooms, sliced thick
3 cups (750 ml) light red wine, such as merlot
1 tablespoon tomato paste
5 bay leaves
1 teaspoon dried thyme leaf
½ cup (125 ml) water
½ cup (125 ml) heavy cream

Cooking

1. Rinse the fish in cold water and pat dry. Season with salt and pepper inside and out and set it aside.

2. Place a long roasting pan (long enough to hold an 18-inch/45-cm fish) over two burners and melt the butter over medium-low heat. Sauté the carrots, celery, and onions until soft, about 15 minutes. Add the mushrooms and cook an additional 5 minutes, stirring gently.

3. Preheat oven to 350°F (175°C). Now stir in the wine, tomato paste, bay leaves, thyme, and water, mix thoroughly, and place the fish on top of the sauce. Cover the pan tightly with a lid or aluminum foil and place in the oven. Bake, undisturbed, until the flesh at the thickest part of the back flakes easily, about 15 minutes.

4. Now comes the hard part. Remove the pan from the oven, and carefully lift the walleye out to a warmed platter. (Two spatulas for the fish and a helper to slip the platter under it will help.) Cover the fish and keep it warm while you finish the sauce.

5. Place the pan back on the stove top over two burners and bring to a simmer over medium heat, stirring constantly, until the pan juices are reduced by about half, 15 minutes. Reduce the heat to medium low, stir in the cream, and cook another 2 minutes until the cream is thoroughly incorporated, hot, and coats the spoon. Remove the bay leaves. Add a bit more salt and pepper to taste if you wish, and serve, spooning the sauce over the whole fish. For individual servings, carefully skin and lift each fillet off the rib cage. Then divide each fillet in half and serve all four portions with a share of the sauce.

Note: If you wish to eat the fish skin-on, it's best to scale the fish—and a spoon works as good as anything else—before you begin step one. If you want to skin the fish after it has been cooked, the skin will peel more easily if you leave the scales on.

ON COOKING WHOLE WALLEYE

When cooking whole walleye, the classic 10-minutes-per-1-inch (-2½-cm) rule has to be bent slightly, in fact, about the same amount of bend as a walleye ribcage. Unlike salmon, trout, bluegill, bass, and many other popular game fish, whole walleye do not lay perfectly flat on the cutting board, ready for you to set a ruler behind them. This is not something you need to worry about with fillets or steaks, where an inch is an inch is an inch.

If you are wondering what I'm talking about, lay out a trout and a walleye, cleaned and ready for cooking. One of the first things you'll notice is the enormous bow in the walleye rib cage compared to the trout's. If you set the ruler up at the back, a 2-pound (1-kg) walleye may have a depth of 2½ inches (6 cm) but it has about half that in thickness of meat. The rest is the Arc de Triomphe, Holland Tunnel, the trajectory of a Cecil Fielder home run. Air, in other words, which doesn't take much time at all to cook.

When you are cooking whole walleye, and to a lesser extent pike, consider the 10-minutes-per-1-inch (-2½-cm) rule, and take your measurement when the fish is lying flat on the counter or cutting board, stuffed if you are stuffing it. But then allow a third of your measurement for wide open spaces and deduct a third of your cooking time. In the Oven-Braised Whole Walleye recipe, you'll notice I cooked a 2½-inch (6-cm) thick walleye in 15 minutes—what would normally be the right time for a fish 1 inch (2½ cm) thinner. The fish comes out perfect in that time—fully cooked, but quite moist and delicious.

NORTHERN PIKE

BARDED PIKE STEAKS

Yield: 2 servings

Barding is the ancient culinary practice of adding fat to the outside of food to give it both flavor and juiciness. Don't get put off by this technical stuff, though. Every filet mignon and London broil steak I've ever seen was wrapped in a slice of bacon—or barded. Pike, with its white flesh and delicate flavor, is a perfect candidate for this kind of kitchen tinkering. And the best part is that if you are camping, or only have a frying pan to cook in, you can turn the seasoned butter baste into the pan, get it good and hot, and fry these bacon-wrapped pike steaks in about 8 minutes. What could be more versatile?

Above: *Barded Pike Steaks, ready for the grill*

Right: *Cut pike steaks with a good sharp knife—or if you are like me and have a little trouble cutting through the spine neatly, use an electric knife.*

Ingredients
2 pike steaks, 1½ inch (4 cm) thick, skinned
2 slices bacon
2 tablespoons butter or margarine, softened
2 tablespoons lemon juice
1 teaspoon salt
½ teaspoon pepper
½ teaspoon sweet Hungarian paprika

Cooking

1. Preheat a propane barbecue on high for 10 minutes, then turn down to medium high. Or start four dozen charcoal briquettes and wait 25 minutes. The fire, on either grill, is ready when you can hold your hand at cooking level for just 4–5 seconds. To adjust the charcoal fire, spread the coals to lower the heat; pile them up to raise it. For both charcoal and propane units, remove the grate from the barbecue and brush or spray lightly with oil to prevent sticking. Since bacon flares easily on the grill, keep a water pistol or spray bottle filled with water beside the barbecue.

2. Rinse the fish in cold water, then pat dry with a paper towel. Wrap a slice of bacon around the perimeter of each steak, tucking in the thin ends, and securing the single layer of bacon with a toothpick. Trim the overlap. Combine the butter and lemon juice in a small bowl. Add the salt, pepper, and paprika and mix well.

3. Brush one side of the steaks with the seasoned lemon butter and place that side down on the grill. Brush the top with lemon butter, and cook about 8–10 minutes to a side, basting two or three times on each side. Turn only once, working gently with a spatula. Cook until the bacon is browned; the fish will be done and still be juicy, too. Serve with baked potatoes dressed with sour cream and chives, or on a bed of sauerkraut.

Barded Pike Steaks: Juicy, delicious, and cooked to perfection.

A Word About Filleting Pike

There are three basic ways to prepare pike for cooking: whole, steaks, or fillets. Filleting is the most popular of the three methods, but leaves the sticky question of the Y bone to contend with. If you don't mind picking bones out of your dinner, follow the universal filleting method. But if you are looking for a way to eliminate the picky mess of bones at the table, you may want to give this new method a try.

First let me introduce you to Scott Sundheim. Scott lives in northeastern Montana, working as a school bus driver by day and a hunting and fishing guide by inclination. His fishing is mostly big lake—Fort Peck to be exact. How large is Fort Peck? Rumor has it that when the dam was finished in 1940 and the lake filled, the sheer weight of accumulated water caused the earth to tip slightly on its axis. Scott plies this mega-mass of water as if it is his own backyard—in his big lake boat, loaded with three motors, two fish finders, a live well generally occupied by a minimum of five species of fish, and his head stuffed with a lifelong knowledge of sun, wind, weather, lures, and days gone bad, good, and dangerous. When it comes to filleting fish, Scott has spent a few moments whittling down the steps.

I fished with him last September. As we pulled into the marina after dark that first day, we had about 40 pounds (18 kg) of pike, walleye, sauger, and bass to take care of. Tired and hungry, I didn't argue when Scott offered to help fillet. But when he placed the fish on its belly and started to fillet from the top, I protested.

"Don't know if anyone else does it this way," he said. "If you like I'll do it the other way. But I won't lose much meat, and you'll end up with larger fillets."

I agreed to let him do one his way, then asked him to gut the rest; at which point I learned that this big macho guy would rather stick his finger in his eye than gut a pike.

"Takes me less time to fillet them," he offered. "But I'll do what you want."

Having cut my teeth on tiny trout streams, and more releasing than keeping, it always leaves me uneasy to be handling more than two or three fish at one time. But I watched, and here's what he did.

Starting with the pike on its belly, and using a very sharp fillet knife, he grabbed the pike by the head and cut straight down through the top of the back just behind the gills to the spine. Then he laid the knife flat to the spine, filleting a chunk of meat off the top of the pike. He stopped at the front edge of the dorsal fin, and removing his knife from the fish, cut straight down in front of the fin to end the fillet. Since the Y bones stop at the front of the dorsal fin, this first fillet was long and thick.

Laying the fish on its side, he then filleted the pike's side—but only the back part, from the front of the dorsal fin to the tail, where there is no Y bone to contend with, leaving the attachment at the tail as an anchor to then skin the fillet. He did the same with the second side.

Once he had those three big fillets set aside, he turned his attention to filleting the sides of the fish below the top fillet. Now here you need to make a decision. Pike larger than 5 pounds ($2\frac{1}{4}$ kg) are more muscled and those flanks make a good-sized fillet for cooking. Fish smaller than 5 pounds ($2\frac{1}{4}$ kg) don't have much of a lower fillet, and the flesh is best saved for croquettes, or soups. As Scott says, "There's not much there to worry about."

I took my fish home, convinced that this new method was slick in the dark, but not sure that it didn't waste a lot of meat. So after a hot shower and a good night's sleep, my husband, John, and I did an experiment. I dug through the cooler and found two fish that looked about the same size. Each weighed just under 5 pounds ($2\frac{1}{4}$ kg) cleaned. I filleted one pike the traditional way, and at the same time, John filleted Scott's way. I was sure we would do Scott's method one time only and never again. The results? To begin with, Scott's method took less time, but it still looked like he had wasted a lot of meat, until I remembered: that night at the lake, he

The sun greets an early morning fly fisherman along the Yellowstone River (Photo © Jeff and Alexa Henry)

had not gutted his fish. Mine was gutted. What looked like a lot of waste on Scott's pike, was nonedible anyway.

But then we tested our work on the scale: John's fish yielded 1 pound 9 ounces (700 g) of meat using Scott's method. My fish yielded 1 pound 15 ounces (868 g) of meat, using the traditional method. But—and it's a big but—Scott's method yielded a much larger fillet: a $\frac{3}{4}$-pound (300 g), 1-inch-thick ($2\frac{1}{2}$-cm) chunk. My largest piece was a $\frac{1}{2}$-pound (250 g) fillet, but it wasn't as solid as John's. I'd had to slice it up to remove the Y bones. And while the tops of a few Y bones protruded from John's big fillet, they were easily removed with a pair of pliers, leaving the flesh whole.

I'm sold. For pike and the Y bone, Scott's method is much more efficient and yields a large fillet suitable for grilling and broiling. I would add one more step, though: After removing the three main fillets on smaller fish, I would take a little time to remove the extra 6 ounces (170 g) of delicious pike in small chunks. Those small pieces would be perfect for any dish calling for small chunks—croquettes, chowders, and mousse, to name a few.

Pike Kabobs Teriyaki

Yield: 4 servings

One of the best things about pike is that the flesh is quite firm—for freshwater fish—which makes it the best fish for kabobs. Don't, however, treat pike as cavalierly as shrimp or halibut in making or cooking kabobs; you still need to use a bit of finesse.

Ingredients
¾ cup (185 ml) soy sauce
3 tablespoons dry sherry
1 tablespoon cooking oil
1 tablespoon sugar
½ teaspoon ground ginger
¼ teaspoon garlic powder
1 tablespoon chopped green onion
2 pounds (1 kg) pike fillets, 1 inch (2½ cm) thick

Preparation
In a small bowl, combine the soy sauce, sherry, oil, sugar, ginger, garlic powder, and green onion. Set this aside until you are ready to cook.

Cooking
1. Cut the pike into 2-inch (5-cm) lengths, and thread two skewers through each chunk, placing the skewers at least ½ inch (1½ cm) apart. If you use wooden skewers, you don't need to soak them in water first: the fish cooks before the wood can catch fire.

2. Preheat a propane barbecue on high for 10 minutes, then turn down to medium high. Or start four dozen charcoal briquettes and wait 25 minutes. The fire, on either grill, is ready when you can hold your hand at cooking level for just 4–5 seconds. To adjust the charcoal fire, spread the coals to lower the heat; pile them up to raise it. For both charcoal and propane units, remove the grate from the barbecue, and brush or spray lightly with oil to prevent sticking.

3. Brush the pike kabobs generously with the teriyaki sauce, then place on the grill. Barbecue about 5 minutes, basting and turning the kabobs twice. The pike is done when it is white but moist looking throughout. Serve as an appetizer with more sauce, or over fried rice.

Note: If you choose to serve the teriyaki sauce with the cooked fish, divide it in half before cooking. Any sauce or marinade that comes in contact with raw fish or meat needs to be brought to a vigorous boil before eating.

PICKLED PIKE

Yield: 1 pound (½ kg)

There seem to be two main methods for preparing pickles: One is to depend on cold vinegar to get the process done; the other gives the vinegar a boost by heating it with the spices and either pouring the marinade over the fish, or even letting the fish cook a bit, before putting the whole works in a jar. Some people don't even use jars, but lay the fish out in a large dish and then cover it with seasoned vinegar.

Fresh dill, by the way, is readily grown in a home garden and rife in farmers markets about the time cucumbers are ready to pickle. Fresh dill is always best with pickles, and pike is a prime pickling fish because of its firm flesh.

Ingredients
1 pound (½ kg) pike fillets
1 onion, sliced thin
1 cup (250 ml) vinegar
1 teaspoon sugar
¼ cup (60 ml) prepared stone-ground
  mustard
3 bay leaves
1 teaspoon black pepper
2 tablespoons chopped, fresh dill tops

Preparation
1. Rinse the fish in cold water, then pat dry with a paper towel. Cut the fillets into bite-sized pieces. Place in one layer in a shallow baking dish or in a glass canning jar. Layer the onion on top.

2. In a small saucepan, combine the vinegar, sugar, and mustard and stir well to dissolve. Over high heat, bring the vinegar to a boil, adding the bay leaves and pepper. Pour the seasoned vinegar over the fish chunks and let cool, uncovered, on the counter. When the marinade is cool, stir the dill in gently, then cover and refrigerate the pickle for 48 hours. It is best when eaten within two weeks.

PIKE CEVICHE

Yield: 8 appetizer servings

If you like fresh garden salads and chilled suppers on hot summer nights, you need to try this classic Spanish dish. *Ceviche* (also spelled seviche) is Spanish for raw fish. But if you watch the fish turn opaque under the influence of the lime juice, you won't be able to tell the difference between cooking with heat and cooking with acid. Be sure however to freeze any raw fish you use for at least 48–72 hours at 0°F (−17.8°C) before using to avoid bugs.

Ingredients

1 pound (½ kg) pike fillets
1 cup (250 ml) fresh lemon juice, about
    4 lemons
1 cup (250 ml) fresh lime juice, about 5 limes
¼ cup (60 ml) orange juice
2 teaspoons green jalapeño Tabasco sauce
2 tablespoons fresh, minced cilantro or
    parsley
2 cloves garlic, minced
1 small red onion, chopped
1 stalk celery, chopped, with leaves
1 cup (250 ml) diced ripe tomatoes
1 tablespoon sugar
½ teaspoon salt
¼ teaspoon black pepper
5 drops red pepper Tabasco sauce, or to taste

Preparation

1. Rinse the fish in cold water, then pat dry with a paper towel. Coarsely chop the fillets and set aside. In a deep, large bowl, combine the lemon, lime, and orange juices, the green jalapeño sauce, cilantro, garlic, onion, celery, tomato, sugar, salt, and pepper. Stir well, then add the red pepper sauce one drop at a time and taste after each drop. Five drops is right for my taste, but add it slowly. You can always add more later at the table.

2. Pour the juice mixture over the fish, toss gently to make sure all the fish is well coated, then cover and refrigerate for 3–4 hours. This both chills the ceviche and "cooks" the fish. Check the bigger pieces of fish to make sure they are opaque throughout before eating. Serve as a dip with tortilla chips.

A no-cook summertime treat: Pike Ceviche

OVEN-BROILED PIKE STEAKS WITH ANCHOVY BUTTER

Yield: 2 servings

In Montana, and perhaps all over the world, the common name for a small pike is a "hammer handle," which gives you a good description of their overall anatomy. If there ever was a fish designed by a steak lover, this is it. Long and of uniform thickness along almost the entire length of their bodies, pike steaked out don't leave many scraps for the soup pot. Just look for a fish with a 3-inch (7½-cm) or deeper rib area, sharpen your knife, and start cutting. Steaks of 1 to 1½ inch (2½–4 cm) thickness cook best. By the way, anchovy paste is a bit pricey, but a little goes a long way, and it lasts forever.

Ingredients

2 tablespoons butter, softened
1 teaspoon anchovy paste
¼ teaspoon onion powder
½ teaspoon lemon juice
2 pike steaks, 1–1½ inches (2½–4 cm) thick
½ teaspoon salt
½ teaspoon pepper

Preparation

Combine the softened butter, anchovy paste, onion powder, and lemon juice, and mix thoroughly with a spoon. Shape into a ball, cover, and chill up to 24 hours.

ON FLAVORED BUTTERS

Both the anchovy butter and curry butter are classic ways to flavor a simply cooked fish. If you don't like curry or anchovies, create your own flavored butter following the basic instructions in these recipes but adding instead 2 cloves of mashed garlic, a tablespoon of prepared Dijon mustard, or a covey of capers if you think fish is too bland. Or make the old standby—and classic treatment for any fish—by flavoring the softened butter with a squeeze of fresh lemon and a few sprigs of minced parsley, if you prefer milder, delicate flavors.

Traditionally, flavored butters are made from all fresh ingredients and shaped into simple forms like balls or log rolls, or fancier hearts, spades, diamonds, and clubs for instance. They are brought to the table chilled, about 1 tablespoon per serving, and placed on the hot, grilled or broiled fish to melt right there in front of you and infuse your dinner and taste buds with vibrant flavors and delicious aromas. Flavored butters can be made 2 hours ahead for immediate consumption, or up to 48 hours ahead of a special occasion. Cover well for 48-hour storage.

Cooking

1. Preheat the broiler and broiler rack for 10–15 minutes. Dry the steaks with a paper towel, brush lightly with cooking oil to prevent sticking, and season with the salt and pepper. Remove the preheated rack from the oven and brush or spray it lightly with oil as well. Replace the rack about 4 inches (10 cm) below the heat, and place the steaks on it.

2. Broil the steaks 5 minutes to a side, carefully turning once with a spatula. The steaks are done when, after a fork is inserted in the thickest part and twisted gently, the flesh flakes easily but still looks moist. Transfer the broiled steaks to a heated dish and place 1 tablespoon of the anchovy butter on each. Serve with cheese-filled ravioli.

*Northern pike
(Photo © Wally
Eberhart)*

Barbecued Pike Fillets with Curry Butter

Yield: 4 servings

Talk about your steaks and whole pike, but it is fillets that fill most people's freezers. So how do you cook fillets on the grill and keep the delicately textured flesh from falling into the coals? Start with leaving the skin on the fillet. This works for all fish fillets from pike to salmon. If your fillets are already skinned, then try laying out a length of aluminum foil on the grill and poking holes all over it with a kabob skewer. Big holes, but not big enough to let the fillet fall through. And if you really have trouble turning that fillet, remember that a fillet of 1-inch (2½ cm) thickness or less doesn't need to be turned. For those really thick fillets, or for people who simply can't stand not having grill marks on both sides, use a hinged grate. And always oil your fish and the grill to prevent sticking.

Ingredients

4 tablespoons butter or margarine, softened
1 tablespoon unsweetened applesauce
½ teaspoon curry powder
¼ teaspoon garlic powder
⅛ teaspoon salt
⅛ teaspoon pepper
2 pounds pike fillets, 1 inch (2½ cm) thick
½ teaspoon salt
¼ teaspoon pepper

Preparation

Combine the softened butter, applesauce, curry and garlic powders, salt, and pepper. Stir well to mix, shape into a ball, and chill 2 hours for immediate use, or make up to 48 hours ahead.

Cooking

1. Preheat a propane barbecue on high for 10 minutes, then turn down to medium high. Or start four dozen charcoal briquettes and wait 25 minutes. The fire, on either grill, is ready when you can hold your hand at cooking level for just 4–5 seconds. To adjust the charcoal fire, spread the coals to lower the heat; pile them up to raise it.

2. Trim the fillets to remove any thin edges, and dry them with a paper towel. Lightly spray or brush the fillets and the cooking grate with cooking oil. (If you are spraying, do it away from the fire.) If you are using perforated foil or a hinged grate, lightly oil those as well. Season the fillet with the salt and pepper.

3. Set the fillets on the grill and cook about 5 minutes a side; if you are cooking fillets with the skin on, start with the skin side down, and let it take the brunt of the cooking time—8–9 minutes. Then quickly turn to give the flesh side a bit of a grid mark. Your fillets are done when you can insert a fork into the thickest part and the fish flakes but is still moist looking. Place a good dollop of chilled curry butter on each serving as it comes off the grill. Serve hot, with mint-glazed carrots: 1 teaspoon each of honey and softened butter, and a sprinkling of mint for each 1 cup (250 ml) of cooked carrots.

PIKE PUFFS

Yield: 8–10 servings

Need an easy-to-make appetizer for your New Year's Day family get-together? Or maybe you need to impress the boss, new in-laws, or just plain give yourself a treat. Try these cheesy, rich-tasting puffs. And if you don't have any pike in the freezer, feel free to experiment. Depending on your tastes, anything—including salmon bits—could fill this bill.

Ingredients

$\frac{1}{2}$ small onion, finely diced
$\frac{1}{2}$ cup (125 ml) mayonnaise
5 tablespoons grated Parmesan cheese
2 tablespoons finely chopped fresh parsley
$\frac{1}{2}$ teaspoon dried leaf tarragon
$\frac{1}{4}$ teaspoon salt
$\frac{1}{4}$ teaspoon pepper
8 ounces (200 g) cooked pike, flaked
5–6 slices white bread

Cooking

1. Preheat oven to 350°F (175°C). In a medium-sized bowl, combine the onion, mayonnaise, and 3 tablespoons of the Parmesan cheese with the parsley, tarragon, salt, and pepper. Mix thoroughly, then fold in the pike bits. Cover and refrigerate while you prepare the toast rounds.

2. Remove the crusts from the bread, and cut each slice into nine squares. Place on a cookie sheet and bake until lightly golden on one side, about 10 minutes. Remove the cookie sheet from the oven, and preheat the broiler. Be sure the rack is about 6 inches (15 cm) away from the heat source, however, for the broiling.

3. Spread 1 teaspoon of the pike mixture on each toast square. Return the squares to the cookie sheet, sprinkle with the remaining Parmesan cheese, and brown lightly under the broiler. Serve hot.

Pike Puffs, an ideal appetizer for Christmas parties or just a Saturday afternoon snack

PIKE-STUFFED CHILI RELLENOS

Yield: 4 servings

Worth the effort!
Pike-Stuffed Chili
Rellenos

I once lived next to a Mexican woman who, out of the kindness of her heart, used to invite me to dinner once a week for homemade chili rellenos. It's still one of my favorite Mexican dishes, and adapts nicely to the firm, white flesh of pike.

Ingredients

6 fresh Anaheim, California, or pablano
    chilies, roasted and peeled
8 ounces (200 g) pike fillet
4 ounces (100 g) Monterey Jack cheese
3 egg whites
$\frac{1}{2}$ cup (125 ml) flour

Cooking

1. Pat the chilies and pike fillet dry with a paper towel. Cut the Jack into twelve thin slices, and the pike into six pieces. In a small bowl, whip the egg whites until they form stiff peaks. (Give the yolks of those eggs to your bird dog to make his coat shine and his heart sing.)

2. In a large skillet, heat about $\frac{1}{4}$ inch ($\frac{1}{2}$ cm) of cooking oil over medium-high heat until hot. Sandwich each slice of pike between two slices of cheese and insert into the chili; fasten with a toothpick if the opening is too large. Roll the chilies in the flour, then in the beaten egg white, getting a good coating of egg on the outside of the chilies even if you have to pat it on with your fingers.

3. Gently place the chilies in the hot oil. Fry until the egg coating is golden brown, 4–5 minutes total, turning carefully with a spatula to brown both sides. Drain on a paper towel while you finish the batch of chilies, and serve hot with Spanish rice, refried beans, and chips.

Fresh peppers are best: Roast them in the oven,
then slip them into a plastic bag for 10–15
minutes to steam them, and they will peel much
easier.

ON ROASTING AND PEELING CHILIES

For chili rellenos, be sure to pick a mild chili. If Anaheim or California chilies are not available, substitute pablanos. All three are large, mild chilies found fresh or canned, depending on where you live and the season. If you can find canned Anaheim or California chilies, they are already peeled. Simply remove the seeds.

Now, to the roasting. The easiest way I've found to peel chilies is to broil them first: Place the chilies on your cool broiler pan, 4–5 inches (10–12½ cm) from the broiler and broil until they are moderately blistered all over. That takes about 4 minutes, but you need to turn the chilies every 40–60 seconds to keep them blistering but not allowing the heat to accumulate in one spot too long. When the chilies are blistered over two-thirds of their area, remove them from the oven, and place in a plastic bag to steam. When the chilies are cool, peel the skin off, leaving the stem for easier handling.

One more step: Make a small slit in the peeled chili and gently wash the seeds out with cold water. If you want, you can freeze the chilies now for later use, refrigerate overnight, or proceed with the recipe right away.

The general rule with chiles: small is hot, large is mild. These Anaheims are perfect for Pike-Stuffed Chili Rellenos—note how big they are compared to the eggs.

PIKE STICKS WITH TARTAR SAUCE

Yield: 6 servings

Make up the tartar sauce and flake mix before you go on your fishing trip, then just fry up the fish when you catch them. Great for bass, pike, and walleye, corn flakes may be the only new wrinkle to fish frying invented by Americans.

The classic fish stick: Pike Sticks with Tartar Sauce

Tartar Sauce Ingredients

½ cup (125 ml) mayonnaise
¼ cup (60 ml) sweet pickle relish
½ teaspoon dry mustard
1 tablespoon lemon juice

Pike Sticks Ingredients

1 pound (½ kg) fish fillets, 1 inch (2½ cm) thick
½ cup (125 ml) evaporated milk
1 cup (250 ml) corn flake crumbs
1 teaspoon celery salt
1 teaspoon onion powder
½ teaspoon dried lemon peel
½ teaspoon black pepper
¼ teaspoon garlic powder
⅛ teaspoon red pepper flakes
Canola or peanut oil for frying

Preparation

1. To prepare tarter sauce: Combine the mayonnaise, pickle relish, mustard, and lemon juice in a small bowl or jar, mix thoroughly, and cover. Chill until ready to use.

2. To prepare the pike sticks: Cut the fish fillets into 1 inch (2½ cm) wide strips. Dry with a paper towel and set aside. Put the evaporated milk and corn flake crumbs into separate shallow bowls for dipping. To the corn flakes crumbs, add the celery salt, onion powder, lemon peel, black pepper, garlic powder, and red pepper. Stir well to mix.

Cooking

In a large skillet over medium high heat, a campfire, or a Coleman stove, heat about ¼ inch (½ cm) of canola or peanut oil to just below the smoking point. When the oil is hot, dredge several fingers of fish in the milk, then the corn flake crumbs, and place in the frying pan. Cook until both sides are golden brown, turning once, about 4–5 minutes. Drain on a paper towel while you finish cooking the rest of your fish sticks, and serve hot, with cold tartar sauce. For an added treat, dredge a few fingers of mozzarella cheese in the milk and corn flakes, and serve them up, too.

PIKE *QUENELLES* WITH GRATIN SAUCE

Yield: 4 servings

A dumpling from the Lyon region of France, *quenelles* are traditionally first boiled in water then baked in a cheese sauce—gratin style. French cookbooks suggest that pike over 4 pounds (2 kg) are good only for hiding in *quenelles* and the classic mousse. Pike was appreciated, though. It was served often on the king's table and stocked in the fish ponds at the Louvre.

Quenelles Ingredients

1½ pounds (¾ kg) diced pike
2 teaspoons salt
½ teaspoon pepper
¼ teaspoon ground nutmeg
3 egg whites
1 cup (250 ml) heavy cream
1 cup (250 ml) milk

Gratin Sauce Ingredients

1 cup (250 ml) heavy cream
2 egg yolks
3 ounces (75 g) Swiss cheese, grated (about
    ¾ cup/185 ml)

Preparation

1. To prepare the *Quenelle*: In a blender or food processor, combine the pike, 1 teaspoon of the salt, the pepper, and nutmeg. One at a time, add the egg whites, processing until the mixture is smooth. Pour into a medium-sized bowl, cover, and refrigerate until the mixture is cold. Return the fish mixture to the blender and add the cream, blending until it is thoroughly incorporated. Add the milk in a steady but slow stream until it is incorporated as well. Chill again until cold.

Cooking

1. Bring a large saucepan of water to a boil, add 1 teaspoon salt. While you are waiting for the water to boil, start shaping the dumplings into ping pong ball–sized portions and set on a lightly floured board until you are ready to cook them.

2. When the water comes to a boil, drop in several of the dumplings, and cook 15 minutes without letting the water come back to a boil. (Lower the heat as necessary; boiling will make the dumplings fall apart.) Drain the dumplings and leave them to cool while you prepare the gratin. Preheat the broiler.

3. To prepare the gratin: Combine the second cup (250 ml) of cream and the egg yolks in a medium-sized saucepan. Stir or beat until thoroughly blended, then place over a burner at medium heat. Bring to a boil, and lower the heat so it stays boiling, but not hard. Stir continuously and cook about 1 minute. Thin with a bit more cream or milk until the sauce coats the spoon. Remove from heat.

4. Arrange the *quenelles* in a lightly buttered baking dish, pour the gratin over the top, and sprinkle with the grated Swiss. Place under the broiler until the gratin is well browned. Serve with garlic toast and a fresh garden salad.

PIKE *ÉTOUFFÉE*

Yield: 6–8 servings

The first Christmas John and I were married was in the middle of a Cajun food craze, and John bought me a Louisiana cookbook. Most of the recipes were too expensive, all of them too hot, so we learned how to adapt them to our palate and creel. This recipe has always been one of our favorites.

When making Pike Étouffée, be sure to brown the oil-flour roux first. Note the deep reddish-brown coating on these vegetables.

Ingredients

¼ teaspoon salt

⅛ teaspoon cayenne pepper

⅛ teaspoon white pepper

½ teaspoon dried basil leaves

¼ teaspoon dried thyme leaf

3 cups (750 ml) fish stock, or chicken bouillon

⅓ cup (80 ml) cooking oil

½ cup (125 ml) flour

½ chopped onion

2 stalks celery, chopped

½ sweet red pepper, chopped

3 tablespoons butter or margarine

2 pounds (1 kg) pike chunks

4 cups (1 liter) cooked rice

Cooking

1. In a small jar, combine the salt, cayenne, white pepper, basil, and thyme. Shake well to mix and set aside.

2. In a saucepan, heat half of the stock to boiling over high heat on a back burner. On the front burner, in a heavy cast-iron skillet, heat the oil over high heat until it just begins to smoke. With a whisk, stir the flour into the oil and keep whisking it until the flour-oil mixture is smooth and turns a deep red brown, about 3–4 minutes. Remove from the heat and add the onion, celery, red pepper, and 1 teaspoon of the spice mix. Stir until the sauce cools down.

3. Add the vegetable mixture to the hot stock, stirring constantly, and cooking until it is all thoroughly mixed, about 3 minutes. Taste the sauce: if you can still taste flour, cook it 1–3 minutes more until you can no longer taste it. Remove the saucepan from the heat and set aside.

4. Wipe out your cast-iron skillet and melt the butter over medium-high heat. Pat the pike chunks dry with a paper towel and quickly sauté them in the butter, about 2 minutes. Add the stock-flour mixture to the sautéed pike, then slowly add enough of the remaining stock to the pan so the sauce pours easily, stirring gently to mix it together. Taste the sauce: add more of the seasoning mixture, to taste. Serve immediately over rice.

Pike Étouffée

Northern pike (Photo © Doug Stamm/ProPhoto)

STUFFED PIKE

Yield: 4 servings

When stuffing a pike, choose one that's larger than a hammer handle, but small enough to fit in your oven—under 4 pounds (2 kg). Allow about 1 cup (250 ml) of stuffing for each 1 pound ($\frac{1}{2}$ kg) of whole fish and allow about 1 pound ($\frac{1}{2}$ kg) of whole, uncleaned fish per person. Remember that all those bones, teeth, and spiky fins take up a bit of weight without adding a bite to the plate.

Ingredients

1 whole pike, 3 pounds (1 $\frac{1}{2}$ kg)
$\frac{1}{2}$ teaspoon salt
1 teaspoon pepper
2 tablespoons cooking oil
6 ounces (150 g) ham, diced
$\frac{1}{2}$ cup (125 ml) diced onion
2 cloves garlic, diced
8 ounces (200 g) morel mushrooms
$\frac{1}{4}$ cup (60 ml) fish or chicken broth

Cooking

1. Rinse the fish in cold water, then pat dry with a paper towel. Season with the salt and a $\frac{1}{2}$ teaspoon of the pepper. Preheat oven to 400°F (205°C).

2. In a large skillet, heat the oil over medium heat. Sauté the ham until slightly colored, then add the onion and garlic, and cook until the vegetables are tender, about 5 minutes. Add the mushrooms to the pan and sauté another 2–3 minutes, tossing to coat the mushrooms. Add the broth and remaining pepper, and continue cooking until the broth has been absorbed. Remove from heat.

3. Place the fish in a lightly oiled baking pan. You may remove the head if necessary to fit the pan, but remember that keeping the body intact prevents moisture from escaping while you cook. Loosely place the stuffing inside the fish, and place in the oven. Bake, uncovered, for 30 minutes. Insert a meat thermometer into the thickest part of the fish, and remove the fish from the oven when the thermometer registers 125°F (52°C). The thermometer will rise 10°F (5°C) more degrees in the first 10 minutes out of the oven; the final temperature should be 135°F (57°C).

4. To serve, remove the stuffing to a heated platter. Then peel the skin off the top fillet, lift the fillet off the spine with a spatula or two, and arrange on the serving platter with the stuffing. Then remove the spine, and lift the second fillet out of the baking pan, carefully turning it skin side up onto the platter. Peel the skin off the second fillet. Serve hot with rice pilaf.

Note: If you cannot find fresh morels, 1 ounce (28 g) of dry morels will make 3 ounces (75 g) of rehydrated ones. No morels at all? Try portabellas.

Perch

Perch Mousse

Yield: 6 servings

It's always nice to have a few things you can do with leftovers, and with mousse, the leftovers almost become more elegant than the original dish. Make this mousse with perch too small to fillet, or any leftover bits—from salmon to walleye to bass. Serve as an appetizer with crackers, or for a main course with a green salad and sourdough rolls.

Ingredients

1 envelope (1 tablespoon) unflavored gelatin
$\frac{1}{2}$ cup (125 ml) water
$\frac{1}{2}$ cup (125 ml) sour cream
2 tablespoons fresh lemon juice
$1\frac{1}{2}$ tablespoons prepared Dijon mustard
12 ounces (300 g) cooked, flaked perch
1 teaspoon dried dill weed
1 cup (250 ml) whipping cream
1 egg white

Preparation

1. In a small saucepan, sprinkle the gelatin on top of the water and let it sit until the gelatin crystals have softened. Heat the mixture over low heat and stir until the gelatin is dissolved. Remove the saucepan from the heat and let the liquid cool to room temperature, about 10 minutes.

2. While you wait for the gelatin to cool, combine the sour cream, lemon juice, mustard, flaked perch, and dill weed in your blender or food processor and purée. Pour the gelatin mixture into the processor and purée another 3–5 seconds to mix thoroughly. Pour into a large bowl.

3. In another bowl, whip the cream until stiff and fold it into the mousse. Rinse your mixer blades, and beat the egg white until it forms stiff peaks. Fold the egg white into the mousse. Pour the mousse mixture into a lightly oiled 4-cup (1-liter) mousse mold or loaf pan. Cover with plastic wrap and refrigerate until set, about 8 hours.

4. To serve, place a plate over the mousse and invert. The light coating of oil should let the mousse slip easily from the mold; if not float the mousse mold in warm water a few seconds, then invert carefully onto a platter. Serve with sliced fresh vegetables and crackers.

SCALLOPED PERCH

Yield: 4 servings

Are you looking for something easy to make? Something that will warm your fingers and toes at the end of a cold winter day? Look no further. If you know how to operate a can opener and turn the oven on, you're good to go.

Ingredients
2 pounds (1 kg) perch fillets
3 tablespoons butter
1 teaspoon salt
½ teaspoon pepper
1 cup (250 ml) canned tomato chunks
1 medium onion, sliced thin
½ cup (125 ml) heavy cream

Cooking
1. Preheat oven to 400°F (205°C). Dry the fillets with a paper towel and place in a lightly buttered baking dish. Brush the butter across the fillets, then season with the salt and pepper. Cover with the tomatoes, then the onion slices. Place uncovered in the oven.
2. Bake about 15 minutes, then pour the cream over the top and bake another 10 minutes or until the sauce is bubbling again. Serve with broccoli florets sprinkled with a bit of lemon and pepper.

Grandfather helps his grandson ready his fishing line (Photo © Alan and Sandy Carey)

Perch *Provençale*

Yield: 4 servings

A simple braise with little fat but lots of flavors for this most delicious fish. There are good reasons people go out and ice fish in February. This is one of them.

Ingredients

¼ cup (60 ml) chopped onion
2 tablespoons cooking oil
3 cups (750 ml) diced tomatoes
3 sprigs fresh parsley
2 sprigs fresh thyme
1 sprig fresh rosemary
1 bay leaf
1 clove garlic, minced
¾ cup (185 ml) dry white wine
¾ cup (185 ml) fish stock or chicken bouillon
1 pound (½ kg) perch fillets

Cooking

1. In a large skillet over medium heat, sauté the onion in the oil until tender but not browned. Add the tomato and simmer gently about 15 minutes. Tie together with string two of the sprigs of fresh parsley, with all of the thyme, and the rosemary sprig, and add along with the bay leaf, garlic, white wine, and stock. Allow these flavors to simmer together, uncovered, for about 15 minutes more to cook down.
2. When you are about ready to eat, gently submerge the perch fillets into the braising liquid and remove the fresh sprigs. Cover and remove from heat. Let sit about 5 minutes while you mince the last fresh parsley sprig. Remove the bay leaf, sprinkle the parsley over the perch, and serve alongside garlic mashed potatoes.

Perch Tempura with Sweet and Sour Sauce

Yield: 4–6 servings

Cook perch by itself in the tempura batter, or make a total tempura—slicing up a tender zucchini, broccoli florets or cauliflower, and some slightly precooked carrot chunks or green beans. And the sweet and sour sauce? I like mine more sour. If you like yours sweeter, add up to twice as much brown sugar while it is cooking.

Tempura Ingredients

½ cup (125 ml) flour
½ cup (125 ml) cornstarch
½ teaspoon salt
1 egg, separated
¾ cup (185 ml) club soda
2 pounds (1 kg) perch chunks

Sweet and Sour Sauce Ingredients

½ cup (125 ml) vinegar
¼ cup (60 ml) packed brown sugar
1 can pineapple chunks with juice, 8 ounces (227 g)
½ red bell pepper, diced large
1 tablespoon cornstarch
¼ cup (60 ml) cold water

Preparation

1. To prepare the tempura batter: Sift the flour, cornstarch, and salt together into a large bowl. Beat the egg yolk in a separate bowl, then gently stir in the club soda. Add the yolk mixture to the dry ingredients, stirring lightly. In a clean bowl, beat the egg white until it forms stiff peaks, and fold it into the batter.

2. To prepare the sweet and sour sauce: In a small saucepan over medium heat, combine the vinegar, sugar, pineapple chunks and juice, and bell pepper and bring to a low boil. Turn the heat down and let this mixture simmer for 5 minutes, until the pepper is soft. Combine the cornstarch and cold water, and stir until all the lumps are out. Slowly stir this mixture into the sauce and continue cooking until it turns shiny, 1 to 2 minutes. Keep warm, or chill to serve.

Cooking

Preheat a deep-fat fryer to 375°F (190°C). Dip four or five pieces of fish or vegetable into the batter and fry until lightly golden, 3 to 4 minutes. The tempura batter will not brown, but the fish and batter will be moist and done anyway. Drain on a paper towel as you continue to cook. Serve with the sweet and sour sauce.

Perch Tempura with Sweet and Sour Sauce

PERCH EGG ROLLS

Yield: 4–6 servings

I prefer my egg rolls with a little hot Chinese mustard, but you can have them plain, with a little prepared hoisin sauce (available in the "ethnic" section of your grocery store), or simply use the sweet and sour sauce from the Perch Tempura (page 61). The wonderful thing about egg rolls is that you can put about anything in them, serve them as dinner or appetizer, and even tiny grocery stores like the IGA in Townsend, Montana, carry them winter and summer.

Perch Egg Rolls

Ingredients

12 egg roll wrappers
1 cup (250 ml) fish or chicken broth
1 tablespoon soy sauce
1 tablespoon dry sherry
1 teaspoon ground ginger
1 teaspoon cornstarch
1 tablespoon cooking oil
8 ounces (200 g) shredded perch
½ cup (125 ml) chopped onion
½ cup (125 ml) chopped celery
½ cup (125 ml) bean sprouts (optional)
1 carrot, coarsely grated
1 cup (250 ml) finely chopped cabbage
1 egg white, lightly beaten
Peanut or canola oil for frying

Cooking

1. Remove the egg roll wrappers from the package and defrost if necessary. Cover with a damp cloth while you work. In a medium bowl, combine the broth, soy sauce, sherry, ginger, and cornstarch. Mix until the cornstarch is completely dissolved.

2. In a wok or a large skillet, heat the oil over medium-high heat. Add the perch, onion, celery, bean sprouts, carrot, and cabbage, and stir fry until the fish is cooked and the onions are lightly browned. Pour the seasoned broth into the hot wok, stir to coat the perch and vegetables, and cook until the sauce begins to thicken. Remove from heat.

3. To assemble the egg rolls, spoon 2–3 tablespoons of the perch filling on the bottom corner of an egg roll wrapper. Roll the bottom corner over the filling, brush the side corners with egg white and fold them over the center. Roll once, then brush the upper corner of the wrapper with egg white, and roll into a tight package. Fill the rest of the wrappers, laying the finished ones on a sheet of waxed paper and covering them with a damp towel while you work.

4. Fill a deep-fat fryer to the manufacturer's recommended depth with cooking oil or put enough oil in a wok to cover the egg rolls. Heat to 375°F (190°C). Gently slip the egg rolls into the hot fat two to four at a time, not crowding them. Fry 3–4 minutes until golden and crisp. Remove with a slotted spoon and drain on a paper towel as you finish cooking the rest of the batch. Serve hot with fried rice.

NEW ENGLAND–STYLE PERCH CHOWDER

Yield: 6–8 servings

Unlike a lot of baby boomers, I never tasted canned soup (or fast food burgers or even Jell-O) until long after I became an adult. My mom believed in making everything from scratch, and to tell you the truth, she was so good at it she ruined me for convenience foods. I walk by those miles of soup cans in the grocery store, and they hold no allure. Tough childhood, eh? Here's one of my mom's favorite soups, made with my favorite fish. You can use pike, walleye, bass, or any other white-fleshed fish, or a combination of fish tidbits leftover from filleting. The chowder base is the same no matter what fish you use, and the best part is that like any fish soup, this chowder is quick to cook.

Ingredients

2 slices bacon
2 large onions, coarsely chopped
1 teaspoon dried leaf summer savory
$\frac{1}{2}$ teaspoon dried thyme leaf
2 bay leaves
4 medium potatoes, diced
3 cups (750 ml) fish stock, or 3 cups (750 ml)
    half-strength chicken stock
1 teaspoon salt
1 teaspoon pepper
2 pounds (1 kg) perch fillet
$\frac{1}{2}$ cup (125 ml) cream
1 cup (250 ml) milk

Cooking

1. In a heavy-bottomed soup pot or Dutch oven of 5-qt (4 $\frac{3}{4}$ -liter) capacity, cook the bacon over medium heat until well browned. Remove bacon from the pot with a slotted spoon and set aside on a paper towel to drain. Add the onion to the fat and cook until golden brown. Stir in the savory, thyme, bay leaves, potatoes, fish stock, salt, and pepper, and cook until the potatoes are tender, about 15–20 minutes. While the potatoes cook, crumble the bacon, and add it to the pot.

2. Prepare the fillets by removing any dark fatty areas, bones, and remnants of skin. Lay the fillets on top of the chowder, and with your cooking spoon, press them under the surface. Cover the pot, remove it from the heat, and let it sit 30 minutes to let the flavors mix.

3. Bring the chowder back up to a simmer over medium to medium-high heat and gently stir in the cream and milk. Remove the bay leaves. Serve as soon as the chowder is hot again, with plenty of saltines.

FISH STOCK

Yield: 1 quart (1 liter)

When it comes to stock—and cooking liquids in general—you are walking in pretty esoteric and philosophical (but also entirely pragmatic and practical) shoes. After all, we all need to eat, but what level of eating do we aspire to? And does that level of aspiration depend more on what night it is and who is cooking than what we *would* eat if all things were possible? It's all part of that wry smile you get when you find out some rich movie star went on this fabulous diet and you could too, if only you buy their book. Except you can't afford to hire a personal chef to cook all your meals. And the best kitchen shortcut you've found lately is a mini-food processor so you don't need to chop onions by hand anymore.

So to stock. If you have the time, fresh stock is the answer. But if you don't have the time or energy to save all your bones and have a pot on the back of the stove all afternoon, there are other options. When it comes to a substitute for fish stock, think pale. White wines, *brut* champagne (the inexpensive stuff works fine), and extra-dry vermouth are traditional fish-cooking liquids, either in partnership with, or instead of, broth. For more oomph, try dry sherry (not the cheap stuff; go for at least the medium price range) for a nutty flavor; Madeira gives fish a fuller, hearty flavor. Oyster sauce, available in the ethnic-foods section of most grocery stores, is a tangy, somewhat sweet addition to give your stir fries real pizzazz. It also goes a long way in soups if you are short on flavored broth. Dry sherry, Madeira, and oyster sauce are concentrated flavors and should be used 1 tablespoon at a time in a large pot. Bottled clam juice, on the other hand, can be used as broth.

I have used beer to brighten a chowder, mixed milk with cream to stretch a sauce, and used lemon and lime juices everywhere. I save shellfish skins in the freezer because they are so strongly flavored they make a quick stock. In short, I cheat any chance I get, but still like to make stock once in a while—usually while the present pot of soup is on the stove—and stick it in the freezer for later. Why? If you don't know, you need to try it.

Ingredients

2 quarts (2 liters) water
3 pounds (1 ½ kg) fish bones (no entrails, gills, or skin)
1 onion
1 carrot, chopped
1 stalk celery, with leaves, chopped
1 bay leaf
10 whole peppercorns

Cooking

1. Place the water in a large soup pot over high heat. Add the fish bones and bring to a rolling boil. Skim off any foam.
2. Add the onion, carrot, celery, bay leaf, and peppercorns, and bring back to a slow boil. Reduce the heat to a simmer, and cover the pot. Simmer for 45 minutes, minimum. If you have more time, let the pot simmer 2–3 hours, with the lid askew.
3. When the water has taken on a light coloration (and remember this is fish—the liquid is not going to be as dark as a beef bouillon), turn the heat off and let the stock cool a bit. Strain the liquid off through a sieve, and discard the solids and spices. Use the stock immediately, refrigerate up to three or four days, or freeze for later. You can freeze the stock in ice cube trays (then transfer to resealable plastic bags when frozen) or measure it directly into plastic freezer bags—1 cup (250 ml) per bag. The stock can be refrigerated four days, then reheated with or without more ingredients, or kept for up to three months in the freezer as is. Use in any recipe calling for fish stock or broth.

Largemouth bass (Photo © Wally Eberhart)

BASS

GRILLED BASS FILLETS WITH GARLIC *AIOLI*

Yield: 4 servings

A summer night, a jug of worms, and thou. Or perhaps a fleece-lined packet of artificial flies. Or silver spangled, purple rubber worms? For a person like me, who sees all possibilities, the choices are mind boggling. But there's no confusion when it comes to *aioli*: it's easy and delicious.

Ingredients

1 cup (250 ml) mayonnaise
2 tablespoons rice wine vinegar
1 tablespoon lemon juice
1 teaspoon dry mustard

5 cloves garlic
2 tablespoons butter or margarine, softened
1 teaspoon salt
2 pounds (1 kg) bass fillets, 1 inch (2 ½ cm) thick

Largemouth bass (Photo © Doug Stamm/ProPhoto)

Preparation

1. In a blender or food processor, combine the mayonnaise, vinegar, lemon juice, mustard, and garlic. Purée 3–5 seconds until the garlic is completely incorporated, with no chunks remaining. Transfer to a small bowl, cover, and refrigerate 1–8 hours.

2. Preheat a propane barbecue on high for 10 minutes, then turn down to medium high. Or start four dozen charcoal briquettes and wait 25 minutes. The fire, on either grill, is ready when you can hold your hand at cooking level for just 4–5 seconds. To adjust the charcoal fire, spread the coals to lower the heat; pile them up to raise it.

3. When the fire is ready, combine the softened butter and the salt in a small bowl and brush one side of the fillets with it. Lay a piece of silver foil on the grate and perforate it all over with a fork. Set the buttered side of the fillet down on the foil, then brush the top side of the fillet. Grill about 7 minutes a side, turning once, carefully. The fillets are done when they flake easily but are still moist looking.

4. Remove from the grill and place on individual plates with a dollop of *aioli* on each piece. Serve with corn bread and fried zucchini chips.

BASS DIJON

Yield: 4 servings

I love dishes that jump up and demand to be noticed, that are hot and dripping with stout sauce, and that stick to your ribs. This one is also good for those other species of pale-meated fish like walleye and pike, so it's not only good, but wears many hats.

Bass fishing in Florida (Photo © Alan and Sandy Carey)

Ingredients

1 ½ pounds (¾ kg) bass fillets
1 teaspoon salt
1 teaspoon pepper
⅔ cup (160 ml) cornstarch
2 tablespoons butter or margarine
½ cup (125 ml) dry white wine
Pinch of allspice
2 tablespoons prepared Dijon mustard
½ cup (125 ml) heavy cream
3 green onions, chopped

Cooking

1. Cut the fillets into serving sizes, and pat dry with a paper towel. Combine the salt, pepper, and cornstarch, and dust the fillets with this mixture.

2. In a large skillet, melt the butter over medium-high heat, and sauté the fillets until brown on both sides, about 7 minutes. Transfer to a heated platter, cover, and keep warm.

3. Pour the wine into the pan drippings and stir the bottom up to get all the flavors. Bring to a simmer, and stir in the allspice, mustard, and cream. Stir constantly, until the sauce thickens just slightly. Pour over each portion of fish and sprinkle with the chopped green onions. Serve with boiled new potatoes tossed with butter and parsley.

THE HEROIC BASS

Yield: 4 servings

I didn't understand sandwiches until I married John. I admit it. I used to take a slice of bologna and slice of cheese and call it food. He has opened my eyes. From peanut butter, banana, and onion sandwiches to heroes that would make Dagwood Bumstead jealous, John believes in the healing power of two slices of bread. I believe this sandwich thing is one of the essential differences between men and women.

The Heroic Bass

Ingredients

1 cup (250 ml) yogurt
1 cup (250 ml) bread crumbs
2 pounds (1 kg) bass fillets, ¾–1 inch (2–2½ cm) thick
2 tablespoons cooking oil
4 tablespoons butter or margarine
1½ teaspoons curry powder
1 red bell pepper, sliced
1 yellow bell pepper, sliced
1 medium sweet Vidalia onion, sliced
4 hard-crusted deli rolls

Cooking

1. Preheat oven to 400°F (205°C). Place the yogurt and bread crumbs in two separate shallow bowls. Pat the fillets dry and cut into four serving pieces. Dip each into the yogurt, then into the bread crumbs, then place on a lightly oiled cookie sheet. Place in the center of the oven and bake 20–25 minutes, until the fillets are opaque and white in color when you poke a fork in one.

2. While the fillets cook, heat the oil in a large skillet over medium heat, and melt the butter in it. When the butter starts to sizzle, add the curry powder, and stir well to mix. Add the sliced peppers and onion, toss to coat with the curry, and turn the heat down to medium low.

Sauté until the peppers are tender, 20–25 minutes, depending on how tender or crunchy you want them to be. The peppers and fish should be ready at the same time, but if not, keep them warm while waiting.

3. To assemble: Lay one fillet on each deli roll and top with the curried peppers and onion. Serve with chips, a large pitcher of mint iced tea—and napkins.

Note: One reason it is so hard to predict how many fish it will take to feed your family is that each fish is different. Some have larger heads, some have better feed. I've seen trout with bellies so big you couldn't hold on to them with two hands, and others so emaciated that their heads seemed twice normal size.

In the case of bass, here's one example. I filleted a bass caught in Florida at the end of February. It weighed $2\frac{1}{2}$ pounds ($1\frac{1}{4}$ kg) on the hook. In the kitchen, I got two nice fillets weighing 12 ounces (300 g), total. (Since bass are a member of the sunfish clan, they share the same muscle pattern: not much meat over the rib cage.) The head of my bass weighed 1 pound ($\frac{1}{2}$ kg), and the rest of the skeleton, skin, guts and fins weighed the same as the fillets, 12 ounces (300 g). Perhaps instead of calling them largemouth bass, we should change the name to largehead.

An angler lands a largemouth bass on a Minnesota lake (Photo © Wally Eberhart)

LARGEMOUTH *VERONIQUE*

Yield: 4 servings

Is there anything more common in a fish recipe than lemon? Perhaps white wine. So it's no big surprise that one of the classic French fish recipes calls for the grapes themselves. Grapes, in fact, are handy little moisture buds to pack in a whole fish when cooking on the broiler or barbecue. Here, we'll use them in a rather delicate but tangy sauce.

Largemouth Veronique

Ingredients

1 ½ pounds (¾ ml) bass fillets
½ teaspoon salt
½ teaspoon pepper
2 tablespoons fresh lemon juice
½ cup (125 ml) extra-dry vermouth
1 tablespoon butter
1 cup (250 ml) seedless green grapes
1 tablespoon cornstarch
1 tablespoon cold water
1 tablespoon undiluted orange juice concentrate
¼ cup (60 ml) heavy cream
1 lemon, cut in wedges

Cooking

1. Cut the fillets into individual serving sizes, season with the salt and pepper. Combine the lemon juice and vermouth and sprinkle over the fish. Let the fillets sit 10–15 minutes.

2. In a large skillet, lay out the fillets, cover with the vermouth and the lemon marinade, and bring to a low simmer. Cook, covered, about 6 minutes, until the fish is opaque. Gently lift the fillets out of the pan, and keep warm.

3. In another saucepan, melt the butter over medium heat. Add the grapes to the butter, tossing gently until the grapes are coated and heated throughout. Remove the grapes from the pan and spoon over the fillets. Now pour the fish pan juices into the butter and bring to a boil. While it heats up, in a small bowl, add the cornstarch to the water and mix thoroughly. Add this cornstarch mixture to the simmering juices, and stir constantly until the sauce thickens. Add the orange juice and cream, stir to mix thoroughly, and when this mixture is hot again, pour over the fish and grapes. Garnish with the lemon wedges, and serve immediately with Brussels sprouts.

BASS JAMBALAYA

Yield: 4–6 servings

It sounds like a soup, but it's a one-pan dinner that takes the boring out of Wednesday night.

Ingredients

1 slice bacon
½ cup (125 ml) chopped onion
½ cup (125 ml) chopped green bell pepper
½ cup (125 ml) chopped celery
4 cloves garlic, minced
1 can whole peeled tomatoes, 28 ounce (795 g)
½ teaspoon paprika
½ teaspoon white pepper
½ teaspoon dried leaf oregano
½ teaspoon dried thyme leaf
⅛ teaspoon cayenne pepper
2 bay leaves
½ teaspoon salt
1 pound (½ kg) shrimp, shelled and cleaned
1 pound (½ kg) bass chunks
¼ cup (60 ml) chopped fresh parsley
4 cups (1 liter) cooked rice

Cooking

1. In a large skillet, fry the bacon over medium heat until crisp, then drain on a paper towel. Pour off all but 3 tablespoons of the bacon fat, and sauté the onion, green pepper, celery, and garlic until the onion is soft, about 4–6 minutes. Add the tomatoes, paprika, white pepper, oregano, thyme, cayenne, bay leaves, and salt. Bring the mixture to a simmer then lower the heat to maintain a gentle simmer for another 20 minutes.

2. To finish the jambalaya: Add the shrimp, bass chunks, and parsley to the simmering pot, and cook until the shrimp is pink and the bass is opaque. Mound your rice on individual plates, and make a bowl in the center of the mound with the back of your spoon. Pour the jambalaya into the rice, and serve.

The early-morning shift at work bass fishing in Florida (Photo © Alan and Sandy Carey)

MARINATED BASS STIR FRY

Yield: 4 servings

What I love about stir fries is that they are quick, whether you make them in a wok or skillet, at home or in the woods on a camping trip. Slice up the vegetables and mix the marinade ahead of time, and all you have to do is catch a fish. And for the rice, campers and other busy people can use instant, saving lots of valuable fuel and fishing time.

Ingredients

⅓ cup (80 ml) Madeira
3 tablespoons cooking oil
1 tablespoon rice wine vinegar
1 tablespoon lime juice
1 tablespoon soy sauce
½ teaspoon ground ginger
½ teaspoon garlic powder
1 pound (½ kg) bass chunks
1 tablespoon cornstarch
1 medium onion, sliced
2 carrots, sliced thin
2 stalks celery, cut into 2-inch (5-cm) lengths
1 cup (250 ml) pea pods
½ cup (125 ml) whole pecans
4 cups (1 liter) cooked rice or Chinese noodles

Angling for bass amid cypress trees (Photo © Bill Buckley/The Green Agency)

Preparation

1. Thirty minutes before beginning the stir fry, combine the Madeira, 1 tablespoon of the oil, the rice vinegar, lime juice, soy sauce, ginger, and garlic powder in a shallow glass baking dish or resealable plastic bag. Mix thoroughly. Pat the chunks of bass dry with a paper towel, then place in the marinade. Refrigerate for 30 minutes. (If you can't start cooking in 30 minutes, be sure to remove the fish from the marinade: it doesn't take long for any fish to absorb a lot of flavor.)
2. Drain the bass chunks and reserve the marinade. Stir the cornstarch into the marinade until it is completely dissolved. Set the marinade and fish aside.

Cooking

1. In a large skillet or wok, heat the remaining 2 tablespoons of oil over high heat. Quickly stir fry the onion, carrots, and celery, until they turn a little brown and the celery is slightly tender, about 3 minutes. Then lower the cooking temperature to medium high, and add the pea pods, bass chunks, and pecans. Toss them all gently together. Continue to stir fry until the bass chunks are opaque, about 2 minutes.
2. Stir the seasoned marinade into the wok, tossing to coat the ingredients well. Raise the heat to bring the sauce to a gentle simmer, then cook until the sauce thickens to the consistency of good turkey gravy. Serve over rice or Chinese noodles.

Smallmouth bass (Photo © Doug Stamm/ProPhoto)

CATFISH

FRIED CATFISH AND HUSH PUPPIES

Yield: 4 servings

If you live or travel in the American South, you soon realize that there are several things you can't get away from: Grits come with every meal; fast food restaurants do a good hush puppy; and, despite bass tournaments, bass boats, and bass plugs, catfish is king. Everyone fishes for them, every restaurant serves them, and everyone has a "secret" recipe for the fry pan. Here's my secret: Use a high smoking point oil like peanut or canola oil, and keep it hot, hot, hot.

Hush Puppie Ingredients

1 ½ cups (375 ml) cornmeal
½ cup (125 ml) flour
1 tablespoon baking powder
½ teaspoon salt
½ teaspoon black pepper
¼ cup (60 ml) finely diced sweet Vidalia
  onion
2 eggs
1 cup (250 ml) milk

Fried Catfish Ingredients

1 cup (250 ml) flour
1 cup (250 ml) cornmeal
1 teaspoon cayenne pepper
1 teaspoon salt
1 teaspoon dried thyme leaf
1 cup (250 ml) buttermilk
1 pound (½ kg) catfish fillets
Peanut or canola oil for frying

Preparation

1. To prepare the hush puppies: In a medium bowl, combine the cornmeal, flour, baking powder, salt, pepper, and onion. In a smaller bowl, beat the eggs and milk together, then stir into the flour mixture. Set this aside while you prepare the catfish.

2. To prepare the catfish batter: In a shallow bowl, combine the flour, cornmeal, cayenne pepper, salt, and thyme. Mix thoroughly. Pour the buttermilk in a second shallow bowl. Fill a large skillet with 2 inches (5 cm) of peanut or canola oil, and heat to just below smoking point.

Cooking

1. To cook the hush puppies: Drop 1 tablespoon of batter at a time into the hot fat and cook for 3 minutes or until golden brown all around. Drain the hush puppies on a paper towel and keep them warm in the oven while you cook the catfish. (It's actually traditional to cook the hush puppies in catfish oil, but I prefer my fish done last as it stays lighter that way.)

2. To cook the catfish: As you finish cooking the hush puppies, begin coating the catfish fillets. First roll them in the cornmeal mixture, then in the buttermilk, and again in the cornmeal. This second time through the cornmeal, press the mixture into the fillet for a good coating.

3. Fry the fillets in the hot oil, turning carefully with a pair of spatulas to keep the oil from splashing, and cook until golden brown on both sides, about 3–4 minutes. If the first one takes much longer than that, you need to raise the heat; the high temperature is needed to seal in the fish's natural moisture and keep the oil out. For a true southern meal, find some field peas and toss them with rice and diced raw red onion.

FILÉ GUMBO

Yield: 4–6 servings

I don't get to chase catfish often enough, living up against the Rocky Mountains. But that doesn't stop me from making gumbo anyway, with bass or any other fish I've got in my freezer. I've even been known to release a few northern pike into the gumbo waters, as well as a few bottom crawlers from the grocery store.

Ingredients

2 slices bacon

2 medium onions, chopped

4 fresh okra, sliced thin

1 pound (½ kg) catfish chunks

1 pound (½ kg) cleaned and shelled shrimp

1 pound (½ kg) crab meat

1 teaspoon dried thyme leaf

1 bay leaf

2 tablespoons filé gumbo powder

1 teaspoon salt

1 teaspoon black pepper

1 tablespoon Worcestershire sauce

1 can of whole, peeled tomatoes, 28 ounces (795 g)

2 quarts (2 liters) fish or chicken stock

Cooking

1. In a 5-qt (4¾-liter) Dutch oven, over medium heat, cook the bacon until crisp. Remove the slices from the pot and set them aside to cool. In the fat, sauté the onions and okra until lightly browned, then add the catfish, shrimp, and crab, and cook until the flesh is opaque. (If you are using imitation crabmeat, add it at the last minute, or it will fall apart and lose any semblance of flavor and texture.)

2. As the vegetables and fish start to brown, add the thyme, bay leaf, filé powder, salt, pepper, and Worcestershire. Toss to coat. Add the tomatoes, with their juices, and the stock, then crumble the bacon strips into the gumbo pot. Stir gently, cover, and bring to a slow simmer. Cook, covered, for about 1 hour. Serve over rice for a main dish, or with crackers for a hearty soup.

SMOKED CATFISH

Yield: Makes 1 pound (½ kg) of smoked fillets

My belief is that for any fish you catch a lot of, you should also have a lot of recipes. So forget that smoking is only for salmon and trout. Catfish, with its unique flavor, is a perfect candidate for the old smoker.

Ingredients

1 pound (½ kg) catfish fillets
⅓ cup (80 ml) sugar
¼ cup (60 ml) non-iodized salt
1 cup (250 ml) soy sauce
1 cup (250 ml) lemon juice
1 cup (250 ml) warm water
½ teaspoon onion powder
¼ teaspoon garlic powder
½ teaspoon white pepper
1 teaspoon green jalapeño Tabasco sauce
3 cups (750 ml) hickory chips

Preparation

1. To prepare the fish: Your results are only good as your raw material, so use fresh fish, cleaned right after catching, then quickly iced down or frozen. Choose the best and firmest-fleshed fish for smoking. Trim thin and torn edges away, and rinse fillets in cold water, then pat dry with a paper towel before brining.
2. To prepare the brine: In a large glass or plastic bowl (do not use aluminum or wood), combine the sugar, salt, soy sauce, lemon juice, water, onion powder, garlic powder, white pepper, and green jalapeño pepper sauce. Stir to

Tools of the trade for smoking fish

mix thoroughly and let cool. Pour into a shallow baking dish large enough to hold the fillets, and immerse the fillets in the brine. Cover with plastic wrap, laying a plate on top if necessary to keep the fish submerged. Refrigerate and let brine 8–12 hours.

Smoking

1. Remove the fillets from the brine solution, rinse, and pat dry. Place on a rack at room temperature to air dry, about 1 hour, or until the surface gets tacky. (The rack allows the air to circulate all around the fillet: use a cake cooling rack or the shelves from your smoker.) Soak the chips in a pan of water 15–20 minutes.

2. While the fillets finish drying, preheat your smoker for 15 minutes. Drain the moisture out of 1 cup (250 ml) of the wood chips and place them over the coals, or in the wood chip pan. When the smoke starts to rise from your smoker, you are ready to cook.

3. Place the air-dried fillets on the shelves of the smoker: put thicker pieces on lower shelves; prop open the rib cage of whole fish for good heat and smoke circulation. Now let the smoker work, adding 1 cup (250 ml) of wood chips at the end of the first hour, then the last cup (250 ml) at the end of the second

hour. That's enough flavor, now let the fillets cook in the smoker another 7–8 hours, 10 hours for whole fish, without opening the door.

4. Cook until the flesh is opaque throughout, 8–10 hours at 140–150°F (60–65°C). Ambient air temperature plays a role, as does relative humidity. We don't have much of humidity around my house, but on a 55°F (13°C) day, it takes exactly 9 hours in my smoker at the temperatures listed above. Colder and wetter days will take longer, warmer and dryer days less time. A properly smoked fish will be cooked, and the skin will peel easily, but the flesh will still have a slightly moist look to it, rather than looking like old, dry shoe leather.

5. Serve immediately on rye bread or crackers, wrapped in a thin slice of Gouda, Swiss, or Gjetost (Scandinavian goat cheese). Store leftovers up to four weeks in aluminum foil or a tightly sealed plastic container; or vacuum pack and freeze it up to three months.

Note: You can reuse the brine two or three times if you store it in the refrigerator between uses and throw it out it in seven days. This way, even if you have a small smoker, you can make lots of smoked fish and save at least one step in the process.

SMOKED CATFISH PÂTÉ

Yield: 2 cups (500 ml)

Like a lot of people, I'm always looking for finger food. It's a question of what's easy. I'll grab a handful of grapes before I'll section a grapefruit and chow down on cookies rather than just fix myself a sandwich. So I guess when I make something like catfish pâté, that's easy and good for me, I feel like a genius. You will, too. Crackers and pâté anyone?

Ingredients
1 cup (250 ml) flaked smoked catfish
1 cup (250 ml) cream cheese, softened
1 teaspoon Worcestershire sauce
1 tablespoon minced green onion
3 drops red pepper Tabasco sauce

Preparation
In a medium-sized bowl, combine the catfish flakes, cream cheese, Worcestershire sauce, green onion, and red pepper sauce. Toss gently, and cover tightly with plastic wrap. Refrigerate 2–4 hours, then taste. Add more pepper sauce if you wish, now that the flavors have developed. To serve, tear open the nearest box of crackers and spread with the pâté.

PANFISH

FRIED PANFISH

Yield: 1 serving, or dozens

Yeah, I know, everyone knows how to fry a panfish. But the point is you can't have a cookbook of classic fish recipes and leave it out. It's simply un-American, like not having hot dogs at a baseball game. So what's new to say? I don't know, but let's say it anyway, starting with defining the creatures.

There are three things a fish needs to qualify for this category: first it has to fit into a pan—without a lot of folderol. The second point is obvious: it has to taste good. And third, it has to be so abundant and easy to catch that the game warden smiles when you walk by with a sackful. Having said that, let's add that when it comes to fixing panfish, there are only a couple of basic anatomical varieties—and, therefore, at least a couple of ways to handle them.

Except for bullheads, which are a small catfish, thus a "round" fish, most panfish are of the sunfish variety—flat, in other words. Flat fish are all built with the vent way forward on the belly, and necessarily, have a large rib cage to hold the viscera in a shortened space. Those rib cages, with their bell shape, don't have much meat on them. The meat on flat fish is across the top two-thirds of the body, and no matter how neatly and quickly you fry them up, the tail is not a delicacy (as in a fried trout).

To prepare flat fish for the pan: The easiest way to handle small flat fish of less than 4 inches (10 cm) across is to dress them, scale them with a scaling tool or the back of a spoon, remove the dorsal, ventral and caudal fins (back, belly, and tail fins), and cook the fish whole. Make V-cuts on both sides of the ventral and dorsal fins to remove the internal base as well as the external fin. And since the most popular way to cook small panfish is frying,

be sure to dust them inside and out with flour, cornmeal, or any dry ground substance of choice to soak up extraneous water. That water, when it hits the hot oil, will splatter—and oil burns are among the most painful.

Larger flat fish more than 4 inches (10 cm) across give you more options. You can cook them as you would smaller panfish, or omit the dressing and just fillet them.

To fillet panfish: Begin by laying the fish flat on a cutting board, and remove the dorsal and ventral fins as above. Lay your knife across the fish, from the back of the skull to the vent. Cut straight down to the spine. (Don't cut through the spine; the head is a handy finger hold for the filleting when left attached.) Using that vent-to-skull line as a guide, lay your fillet knife parallel to the cutting board and slide it between the fillet and the rib cage. Keep on filleting at that diagonal up and across the fish until the fillet is free. Now lay the fillet flat on the cutting board, scale side down, and slice the fillet off the skin. Do the same with the second fillet. Discard the tail, head, and still-enclosed viscera.

For bullheads: The trouble with bullheads, like catfish, is that you don't eat the skin. And since most bullheads are too small to fillet, they're a bit more work than flat fish to prepare.

Begin by skinning the bullhead as you would a catfish: With the fish on its belly, lay your knife behind the adipose (the rear back) fin, and cut the skin across the top of the back. Stop at the dorsal (the forward back) fin, and cut down to the spine. Leave the head attached.

Pick the fish up now and bend the head down against the chest, breaking and splitting the backbone at your dorsal cut. Place your

right hand over the opening into the rib cage, grasping the head with your left. Slowly pull the head down the belly-side toward the tail, peeling the skin and drawing the viscera out with one motion.

Finish the cleaning job by rinsing the chest cavity, and removing the kidneys (the red line on either side of the spine). Now you can cook the "whole" bullhead any way you wish. Larger bullheads, if you are lucky enough to find them, can then be filleted as well.

To fry panfish: Pour about 1 inch (2½ cm) of oil in a heavy-bottomed skillet. Heat the oil to the point where you see smoke begin to swirl off the top, then reduce the heat a bit so the smoking quits. That means you must fry fish in oils with a high smoking point like canola and peanut oils. Then dust the fish and cook them quickly until they're golden brown on each side. If you need to add more oil, do it while the pan is empty of fish, then get it hot again before you resume cooking. And don't overcook these wafer-thin delicacies. If you want to know how fast fish cooks in hot liquid, try taking a chunk of fish and tossing it into a pot of boiling water. It will be moist and cooked in seconds. No need to make it a marathon.

The final question is, How many panfish are enough? The answer is, Who knows? While most experts recommend 1 pound (½ kg) of whole fish per person, I don't notice those same experts writing many sunfish cookbooks. And of course there's always the question of how much more do we eat when we've spent our days catching naive little fish and our nights sleeping under the stars. My advice? Cook lots. We all eat more in the outdoors, and it all tastes better than anything we ever cooked at home.

A youngster casts for fish off Gull Point in Yellowstone Lake (Photo © Jeff and Alexa Henry)

Stuffed Mushroom Caps

Yield: 16 mushroom caps

Make stuffed mushroom caps with any fish you have—even salmon and trout—but pale-fleshed fish is my favorite. And make the caps with those ordinary, common, run-of-the-mill mushrooms that are always available at your grocery store. Just buy fresh, and pick the best ones. Serve as an appetizer, or just to give yourself a treat.

Stuffed Mushroom Caps

Ingredients

16 mushrooms (about 8 ounces/200 g), about 2 inches (5 cm) diameter each
3 tablespoons butter
2 ounces (50 g) panfish fillet, finely chopped
½ cup (125 ml) bread crumbs
1 tablespoon fresh minced parsley
1 tablespoon chopped green onions (greens only)
2 tablespoons finely chopped cucumber
¼ teaspoon dried basil leaf
½ teaspoon salt
½ teaspoon pepper
1 egg, lightly beaten
½ cup (125 ml) grated Parmesan cheese

Cooking

1. Remove the mushroom stems and finely chop them. Gently rinse and dry the caps and set them in a lightly buttered shallow baking dish.
2. In a large skillet, melt the butter over medium heat and lightly sauté the chopped stems, panfish bits, bread crumbs, parsley, onions, cucumber, basil, salt, and pepper until the fish is opaque, about 2–3 minutes. Remove from the heat and stir in the egg.
3. Preheat oven to 375°F (190°C). Brush the caps inside and out with a bit of melted butter, and fill each with some of the panfish filling. Sprinkle with the Parmesan cheese. Bake in the center of the oven for 15 minutes, until the caps are lightly browned and tender, and the cheese has melted. Serve hot, with other appetizers like raw vegetables with ranch dip, smoked salmon, and liver pâté.

PANFISH ENCHILADAS

Yield: 4–6 servings

Make these Mexican classics with panfish, or, if you've got some other leftover pale-meated fish, don't be afraid to mix, match, or switch.

Ingredients

1 tablespoon cooking oil
1 pound (½ kg) panfish chunks
1 teaspoon red chili powder
1 teaspoon ground cumin
6 green onions, diced
1 tablespoon lemon juice
⅓ cup (80 ml) sour cream
2 tablespoons chopped fresh cilantro
1 teaspoon salt
½ teaspoon black pepper
4–6 flour tortillas, 8 inches (20 cm) diameter each
2 cups (500 ml) red salsa
¼ pound (100 g) Cheddar cheese, grated

Cooking

1. In a large skillet, heat the oil over medium-high heat and sauté the fish chunks with the chili powder and cumin until the fish is opaque, about 4 minutes. Remove from the heat and stir in the onions, lemon juice, sour cream, cilantro, salt, and pepper. Set aside.

2. Preheat oven to 400°F (205°C). In a lightly oiled baking pan, lay out one tortilla. Spread 1 tablespoon of red salsa over the tortilla, then spoon a quarter of the seasoned fish mixture down the center of the tortilla. Roll up to one end of the baking dish, with the seam side down. Do the same with the rest of the tortillas, then sprinkle the remaining salsa across them and top with the cheese.

3. Place the enchiladas, uncovered, in the center of the oven and bake for 15–30 minutes until the insides are piping hot and the cheese is melted. Serve with refried beans.

Note: You can use bottled salsa, or make this simple recipe from scratch. For each ripe tomato, use 1 roasted and peeled jalapeño pepper and 1 medium-sized onion. Chop by hand for chunky salsa, or in the food processor for a finer chop. Chill and serve. Makes about 2 cups (500 ml). To store, can as for stewed tomatoes.

This is the recipe I use for canning when my tomatoes are ripening too fast to eat fresh. It is a wonderful treat to have in the pantry and one you'll reach for even more than the stewed tomatoes. If you're making the salsa fresh for immediate use, add 1 teaspoon fresh minced cilantro for an exotic touch—and to make it really fast, omit the roasting and peeling and just use canned, whole jalapeños. Personally I think it's the fresh, ripe tomato that makes this salsa.

Bluegill (Photo © Doug Stamm/ProPhoto)

BLUEGILL CHIPS

Yield: 2 servings

My friend Jim lives in Florida and is quite adept at catching bluegills large enough to fillet. Rumor has it he likes to catch alligators on bass plugs, but I have no proof of that. I do have proof of big bluegills, though: He Fed-Exed me a brace of magnificent blues last February. If you are lucky or skilled enough to catch big panfish of any variety, here's a great way to cook them without bones. By the way, I've done this recipe with eight fillets because the last bluegill I weighed was 8 ounces (200 g) on the hook, and provided two fillets of 1 ounce (28 g) each. Eight fillets for two people should provide 4 ounces (100 g) of animal protein per person.

Bluegill Chips

Ingredients
8 panfish fillets
Peanut or canola oil for frying
1 egg, lightly beaten
1 cup (250 ml) white cornmeal
2 teaspoons coarse salt
1 teaspoon pepper

Cooking
1. Pat the fillets dry with a paper towel and set aside. Pour ¼-inch (½-cm) of oil into a large skillet, and heat just short of the smoking point. Put the egg and cornmeal in separate shallow bowls. Dip the fillets in the egg, then in the cornmeal, and slide into the hot oil one at a time. (This keeps the oil hot, so the fillets cook quickly without absorbing unnecessary oil.)

2. Fry until golden brown on both sides, about 1–2 minutes for ¼-inch (½-cm) thick fillets, flipping once, and drain on a paper towel while you finish cooking the other fillets. Sprinkle with the coarse salt and pepper while the fillets are still hot, so the salt sticks—like real chips. Serve for breakfast with hash browns, orange segments, and lemonade; or for lunch with potato salad and corn chips.

SUNFISH MACARONI AND CHEESE

Yield: 4 servings

When my son was little I used to cook up one of those ubiquitous boxes of mac and cheese, then turn a can of tuna into it. It was one of his favorite dishes. But since I've gotten better at catching a reliable stringer of fish, this old favorite has improved considerably. It's now fresh fish instead of canned. And the cheese? It's become a three-cheese extravaganza. By the way, you should use your favorite panfish and your favorite pasta: I like rotelli because its corkscrew shape holds a lot of the cheese sauce.

Ingredients

1½ cups (375 ml) milk
4 tablespoons flour
4 tablespoons butter or margarine
1 teaspoon curry powder
½ cup (125 ml) grated Cheddar cheese
½ cup (125 ml) grated Swiss cheese
½ cup (125 ml) grated Muenster cheese
4 cups (1 liter) cooked rotelli pasta
8 ounces (200 g) flaked and baked sunfish
2–3 tablespoons bread crumbs (optional)

Cooking

1. Combine the milk and flour in a 1-quart (1-liter) microwaveable bowl, stir the flour until it is dissolved, then add the butter. Microwave for 2 minutes in a 500-watt oven, 1 minute in a 700-watt unit. Remove and stir. Return to the microwave and cook about 2 more minutes, stirring two or three times, until the sauce bubbles up and begins to thicken.

2. Preheat oven to 350°F (175°C). Remove the sauce from the microwave and stir in the curry powder, ¼ cup (60 ml) each of the Cheddar, Swiss, and Muenster cheeses, rotelli, and the flaked fish. Sprinkle with the rest of the cheese, and 2–3 tablespoons bread crumbs if you wish. Bake, uncovered in the middle of the oven, 40 minutes, until the cheese bubbles. Serve immediately with peas and carrots.

COLD-WATER FISH

TROUT

If taste were all, I'd live along the eastern seaboard and trap crab and lobster for my supper. But, the truth is I love the small mountain streams of the west; the quiet of unpopulated places; the wind in the pines; the accidental sighting of a whitetail deer, owl, bobcat, or great blue heron in the corner of my eye—or in my back cast. I'd rather eat crab, but I'd rather see rainbow trout jumping at rod's length and feel the primeval jerk of a big brown hanging under a crumbling cutbank.

I live in trout country. Country defined by fast, cold water. I have rainbows and browns in my backyard; lake trout just north of me. Top out over Ridge Road into the next creek drainage—we're talking a short dusty hop in a pickup truck, not the Continental Divide here—and there's brook trout. Seventy miles (112 km) to the nearest cutthroat lake, farther to a natives-only creek. Rare golden trout live in lakes too far for my asthma to take me easily, but they are there for the taking. And if you don't catch one under the big sky, just go into any gift shop and there are trout-shaped Christmas ornaments, telephones, hot mitts, lamp bases, sterling silver or enamel-painted earrings, pins, and bracelets. Kitchen shops carry trout napkin holders and poaching pots in three sizes; mousse pans (but *moose* require a permit drawing) come in the shape of casually swimming and leaping rainbows.

Rainbow trout (Photo © Doug Stamm/ProPhoto)

Our house is trout friendly, rustic casual. Not much pine furniture or colonial blue plaid, but there are generally three pairs of waders drip-drying on the side of the barn, at least one creel hanging from a handy pine branch, and fishing vests—summer and winter varieties—hang year-round in our mud room. (Our two Labrador retrievers are trained to fish—namely they don't retrieve lures or jump into pools.) I wrapped the biggest trout I took last season, whole, in freezer paper and haul it out for visitors when they doubt I'm telling the truth. (A large pike is similarly wrapped and man-handled.)

We don't fish often enough. There's a stretch of the Missouri River we've been talking about floating for seven years and haven't gotten to yet. But we fish our backyard stream after we're done working, instead of making a commute home. That's two hours wading—not riding—in high-top sneakers in August, hippers most days, always catching something because we've come to know the stream not just by its seasons, but by its days. I'm sure there are better fish to eat, shellfish for instance, but trout have a centuries-old mystique and culinary tradition unrivaled by any other finned fish. Most important, though, I can't imagine any better way to live.

Here are a few delicious, and time-honored, ways to prolong a day of trout fishing.

Previous page: *Rainbow trout (Photo © Doug Stamm/ProPhoto)*

TROUT ALMONDINE

Yield: 4 servings

Make trout almondine at home on a cold winter's night, or stash a handful of almonds, a lemon, and a couple of sprigs of parsley in the cooler next time you go on an overnight fishing trip. This dish may sound snooty and continental, but it cooks up quickly over a campfire, Coleman stove, or your kitchen range.

Trout Almondine

Ingredients

2 trout, 12 inches (30 cm) long each
Salt and pepper, to taste
½ cup (125 ml) flour
4 tablespoons butter or margarine
4 ounces (100 g) slivered almonds
2 tablespoons fresh lemon juice, about
   ½ lemon
2 tablespoons chopped parsley

Cooking

1. Rinse the trout in cold water and shake gently to remove excess moisture. Do not dry the trout. Lightly sprinkle the inside of the trout with salt and pepper to taste, then dust the outside with the flour and set aside.

2. In a large skillet, melt 2 tablespoons of the butter over medium-high heat until the butter is hot but not darkening, and quickly brown both sides of the trout. Then lower the heat and cook the trout 10–12 minutes, turning once. Drain the cooked trout and place on a heated platter.

3. Melt the rest of the butter in the skillet over medium heat and add the slivered almonds. Shake the pan back and forth until the almonds are golden brown. Add the lemon juice and chopped parsley, and remove from the heat. Stir gently, then spoon over the trout and serve immediately. Serve with boiled new potatoes, and if you like lots of lemon, slice the second half of that freshly squeezed lemon into wedges.

Note: If you think flour, cornmeal, and other dry coatings are just adding flavor and calories to your fish, think again. There are few things harder to get totally dry than a trout. If you didn't roll the fish in something powdery and dry to soak up all the microscopic droplets of water, you would be in grave danger from oil flareups in the pan. Fish are best cooked at high temperatures, and hot oil on your skin is quite painful.

POACHED TROUT WITH HORSERADISH CREAM

Yield: 2–4 servings

Daybreak on Oregon's Mann Lake (Photo © Dennis Frates)

Poaching has always been a great way to cook large fish—and you don't have to take my word for that. Just look in any kitchen supply store: the smallest poaching pan is 18 inches (45 cm) long, and the size expands rapidly from there. The advantage of the poaching pan is the lift-out tray, making fish handling easy. But you don't need a dedicated poaching pan. James Beard, the great gourmet of my parents' generation, remembers that his family kept a baby's bathtub to prepare the larger fish. Use what you have, then wrap the fish in cheesecloth for easier handling and curve it to fit the pan. If necessary, remove the head to make the fish fit. After all this is a water bath: there is no danger of drying out the fish.

Horseradish Cream Ingredients

¾ cup (185 ml) heavy cream
¼ cup (60 ml) white wine vinegar
2 tablespoons grated fresh horseradish
Salt and pepper, to taste

Poached Trout Ingredients

1 onion, sliced
1 carrot, sliced
1 stalk celery, with leaves, coarsely chopped
1 tablespoon dried thyme leaf
2 bay leaves, crushed
1 bunch parsley

2 cloves garlic, whole
2 teaspoons peppercorns
2 teaspoons salt
2 cups (500 ml) dry white wine
1 quart (1 liter) water
1 whole trout, 18 inches (45 cm) long

Preparation

1. To prepare the horseradish cream: Beat the cream until stiff, then gradually beat in the vinegar until the mixture has the consistency of mayonnaise. Fold in the horseradish and season with salt and pepper to taste. (If you do not have any fresh horseradish, you can substitute an equal amount of cream-style prepared horseradish, just reduce the vinegar by 1 tablespoon.) Cover and chill 1–2 hours.

2. To prepare the poached trout: Combine the onion, carrot, celery, thyme, bay leaves, parsley, garlic, peppercorns, salt, wine, and water in the poacher. Bring the mixture to a boil, then reduce the heat and simmer slowly for about 45 minutes. If the fish is refrigerated, place it on the counter, and allow it to come to room temperature before poaching.

Cooking

1. Gently place the fish in the simmering court bouillon, and when the liquid again reaches the boiling point, turn the heat down and start your timer allowing 10 minutes per 1 pound (½ kg) of fish. You don't want to boil the fish; poaching is a gentle process that balances between keeping the water at the boiling point, but not allowing it to rock and roll the fish, thus making it fall apart. A few bubbles here and there are ideal.

2. The fish is done when the flesh lifts cleanly off the bones. Gently remove it from the poaching liquid as soon as it is done. Place the trout on top of a couple of layers of paper towels on a platter to absorb excess liquid as it drains. Serve hot, or allow to cool to room temperature, then seal in plastic wrap and chill overnight for a cold entrée. Either way, serve with a generous dollop of horseradish cream.

Note: To properly poach any fish, you need to just cover the fish with court bouillon. So how do you know how much bouillon is enough, before it's boiling? The easiest way I know is to hold a rehearsal. Lay your fish in the poaching pan, on its side as you will for cooking. Now, gently, run cold tap water into the pan until the fish is covered. Remove the fish and measure your liquid. In my 18-inch (45-cm) pan with an 18-inch (45-cm) trout, the combination of water and other ingredients given in this recipe was just enough. If you find you are off by a small amount, simply dip out, or add a bit of liquid (1 part wine, 2 parts water).

PAN-FRIED TROUT IN CORNMEAL WITH POTATO PANCAKES

Yield: 2 servings

The trick to good pan-frying is to turn the heat up. The best results come from oils with a high smoking point—the temperature at which your pan starts to smoke, and your fish turns black, even though it isn't burned. Peanut oil is best, but canola also has a high smoking point, is cheaper, and is lower in saturated fat. Butter, margarine, lard, and olive and corn oils won't work as well because of their low smoking points. Finally, have the fish at room temperature before you put it in the pan, so the trout itself doesn't cool the pan.

Two reasons you roll fish in cornmeal: It adds flavor, and it soaks up water that would spatter and burn the cook when frying in hot oil.

Ingredients

4 pan-sized whole trout
1 cup (250 ml) cornmeal
3 large red potatoes
1 small onion
1 egg
2 tablespoons flour
½ teaspoon salt
½ teaspoon baking powder
Peanut or canola oil for cooking

Preparation

1. Rinse the trout, and shake off the excess moisture. Do not towel dry. In a shallow bowl, dredge the trout in the cornmeal, then set aside (partly to allow it to warm to room temperature, partly to prepare the potato pancakes).
2. To prepare the pancakes: Coarsely grate the potatoes and onion into a large bowl. Stir the grated potato and onion together, then pick up a fistful of the mixture, squeeze, and discard the excess moisture. (Don't do a Schwarzenegger, just get the easy stuff.) Do the same with the rest of the mixture. Stir in the egg. Combine the flour, salt, and baking powder, and add to the bowl. Stir well to mix.

Cooking

1. This all cooks up fast and can be made in one pan, starting with the potato pancakes. Using a heavy-bottomed skillet, pour $\frac{1}{4}$ inch ($\frac{1}{2}$ cm) of canola or peanut oil in the pan. Heat the oil on medium high, then drop the batter 1–2 tablespoons at a time into the hot oil. Cook until golden brown, about 2–3 minutes a side. Drain on a paper towel as you go.

2. When all the potato pancakes are made, add enough oil to the pan to bring it back up to $\frac{1}{4}$-inch ($\frac{1}{2}$-cm) deep. Raise the heat to high. Dredge the trout in cornmeal one more time while you wait. The cornmeal not only adds flavor to the trout, but absorbs moisture so the hot oil doesn't pop when you gently set it in there.

3. Test the oil: it's ready when a bit of cornmeal dropped in the pan immediately starts to brown. Holding the trout by the tail, gently lower them into the pan one at a time. The oil will be deep enough to come about halfway up the body and lap slightly over the belly flap. Cook on high, about 1 minute to a side. (It doesn't sound like enough time, but you'll notice when you turn the fish after that first minute that the cooked rib cage has expanded, and stands out. That's a sign that it is cooked enough.) Carefully, remove from the oil, drain on paper towels, and serve immediately. The potato pancakes can be served with applesauce or, like hash browns, with ketchup.

Note: If you have been adventurous enough to go to where the golden trout live, and have one in hand, the best thing is to enjoy your catch right where you are. Golden trout are higher in fat content than other trout, and since it takes a long walk to get to their water, keeping them fresh is a problem. Best not to try to tote them out but simply enjoy them in camp. You can carry almonds and fresh parsley almondine al fresco, or cook them camp-out style as with this recipe.

Pan-Fried Trout in Cornmeal— better known as Campout Trout— with a side of potato pancakes

SMOKED TROUT

Yield: 5–20 servings as appetizers

This is one of the most versatile recipes in any angler's repertoire. If you like smoking, you can smoke any fish, any size, at any time of the year (providing the ambient air temperature is above freezing or you have a heated shed for the smoker), and the amount you smoke at one time is limited only by how proficient your angling and how large your smoker. Having said that, I will admit that I prefer to smoke oily fish, mostly because the flakier, lighter fish are delicious so many other ways. In this, I follow the classic, age-old rule of what to smoke, if only by default. Salmon, whitefish, and trout are the prime smokers, but if that's not what you catch, bass, catfish, and even, gulp, walleye are quite good smoked.

Brining the trout before smoking it

Ingredients

1 quart (1 liter) warm water
½ cup (125 ml) non-iodized salt
½ cup (125 ml) sugar
1 teaspoon whole mustard seeds
1 teaspoon whole peppercorns
5 pan-sized trout, whole
3 cups (750 ml) hickory or alder chips

Preparation

1. Combine the water, salt, sugar, mustard seeds, and peppercorns in a large jar. Mix or shake well until the salt and sugar are dissolved, then let the brine cool to room temperature. One quart (1 liter) yields enough brine to fill a 10x6-inch (25x15-cm) dish 1½ inches (4 cm) deep once the fish are added. This is plenty deep for pan-sized trout, and you can make more or less brine to accommodate your dish and creel.

2. While the brine cools, rinse the fish in cold water, then pat dry inside and out with a paper towel. Place them in a non-corrosive, shallow baking dish just large enough to hold your fish. Pour the brine over the top, cover the dish with plastic wrap, and refrigerate 12 hours, turning the fish occasionally. Since fish, even when dead, have a tendency to float in water, you may have to place a saucer over the plastic wrap to keep the trout submerged.

3. Remove the fish from the brine, rinse in cold water, then pat with a paper towel. Allow to air dry at room temperature for 1–2 hours until the flesh is slightly sticky. (I remove the racks from the smoker to air dry the fish.) The trout is now ready for the smoker.

Smoking

1. For an electric smoker, soak your wood chips in water for 15–30 minutes, then drain off the excess liquid before using. Drain 1 cup (250 ml) of chips and add them to the smoker pan to begin with. Place the chip pan in the smoker, turn the smoker on, and wait 15 minutes, or until the first sign of smoke appears. When the smoker is ready, place the fish on shelves as far from the heat as possible, or hang from a hook or string looped over a bar. Prop open body cavities with a couple of toothpicks. For moderate smoke flavor, 3 cups (750 ml) of chips is enough, added 1 cup (250 ml) at a time in the first three hours of smoking.

2. Cook until the flesh is opaque throughout, 8–10 hours at 140–150°F (60–65°C). Ambient air temperature plays a role: on a 55°F (13°C) day, a 10-inch (25-cm) trout takes about 9 hours in my smoker at the temperatures listed above.

Colder days, especially windy ones, will take longer; warmer days, less time.

3. Serve immediately on crackers with cream-style horseradish, or shredded over an August afternoon salad topped with your favorite Italian dressing. Store leftovers up to four weeks in the refrigerator in aluminum foil or a tightly sealed plastic container; or vacuum pack and freeze it up to three months.

Note: If you have large fish to smoke, fillet them out, or cut into chunks to fit the width of your brining dish. Leave the skin on for easy handling. And recycle your brine: It can be used up to three times in one week if kept refrigerated, or doubled and tripled in volume to handle large numbers of fish. Just be sure you load the smoker loosely, allowing the smoke to circulate on all sides, and inside, of the fish to ensure proper cooking.

GENERAL RULES FOR SMOKING

1. Use only fresh fish. If you have to hold the fish a while before smoking, freeze them immediately for later use.

2. Leave the skin on fillets and whole fish to make handling easier. The skin also protects the outer flesh from drying out before the inner flesh is properly cooked.

3. Tradition says fatter fish make better smokers. The fat absorbs more of the smoke flavor and keeps the flesh from drying out. But if you like smoked fish, and prefer catching catfish, bass, or pike, smoke on. The smoking tradition grew in places that had an abundance of oily fish—use what you have in abundance and create a new regional tradition.

4. Alder is traditional for salmon, hickory for a stronger smoke flavor. Fruitwoods are not as traditional, but cherry, apple, and peach woods add a mellow flavor to smoked foods. Soak chips 15–30 minutes before smoking, and never use resinous woods like pine as the sap will leave a bitter flavor. Mesquite will also leave a bitter flavor when used continuously for long cooking. A little at the start goes a long way.

5. To predict cooking time, check the temperature of your smoker with a common oven thermometer. It's best to do it on a dry run—without wood smoke to gum up your readings. Just plug in your smoker, first time you use it, with an oven thermometer in it. Then check it now and then, over the years, in the last 2 or 3 hours of smoking, after the wood chips are done. Your smoker should operate at 140–150°F (60–65°C). Alter the cooking time if your smoker deviates from that norm.

6. Your fish is done when the flesh is opaque, and you can pull the skin off easily. It should still look moist, however. The whole purpose of cooking at this temperature is to keep the flesh tender.

7. To store your smoked fish, let it cool to room temperature, then wrap in plastic bags. It will keep in the refrigerator for four weeks, or in the freezer three to six months.

TROUT *MUNIERE*

Yield: 4 servings

If you have an abundance of pan-sized trout, use them whole. Large trout? Fillet them out, and they'll be just as good. But, in the true meaning of a classic recipe, you don't need to use trout at all. Perch, whole or filleted, or any other white-meated fish will work as well.

Angling for trout in a Montana creek (Photo © Alan and Sandy Carey)

Ingredients
4 pan-sized whole trout, or 4 fillets
½ cup (125 ml) milk
¼ teaspoon salt
1 cup (250 ml) flour
¼ teaspoon pepper
Peanut or canola oil for frying
3 tablespoons butter
1 lemon
2 tablespoons minced parsley

Cooking
1. Rinse the fish in cold water, then pat dry with a paper towel. Combine the milk with the salt in one shallow bowl, and the flour and pepper in another. Dip the fish in the milk, then dredge in the flour. Let them sit in the flour—and warm to room temperature if they were in the refrigerator—while you heat the oil.

2. In a skillet large enough to hold the fish without crowding, heat ¼ inch (½ cm) of peanut or canola oil over high heat, but do not let it smoke. Brown the fish on both sides, about 1–2 minutes a side for panfish and fillets less than 1 inch (2½ cm) thick, then remove to a warm platter.

3. Pour the oil off the skillet, and add the butter. When the butter starts to brown, pour it over the fish. Now, slice the lemon in half and squeeze the juice of one half over the fish. Sprinkle with parsley, and serve immediately with the second half of the lemon sliced as garnish and a generous helping of corn on the cob and fresh, hot garlic bread for everyone.

Rainbow trout (Photo © Wally Eberhart)

PICKLED TROUT

Yield: 1 quart (1 liter)

There's something about a jar of fish pickled with the skin on that brings out the eighth of Norwegian in my husband John's ancestry. (Where he gets his Irish on St. Patty's day has something to do with married people getting more alike as the years go by.) Fillet and chunk up a large fish, or use "saddles" with this nifty method of boning. Please check the recipe note, however, and use only fish that have been frozen.

Pickled Trout

Ingredients

1 red onion

1½ cups (375 ml) vinegar

Dash of salt

20 peppercorns

2 bay leaves

4 pan-sized trout, whole

4 sprigs fresh dill, about 4 inches (10 cm) long

Preparation

1. Peel the onion and slice it thinly into rings. In a medium saucepan, bring the vinegar, salt, peppercorns, and bay leaves to a boil. This boil only takes 1–2 minutes to achieve on high heat, but be sure not to breath in the fumes. Set the marinade aside to cool.

2. Rinse the trout and pat dry. With a poultry shears, extend the belly cut down through the vent to the tail. Lay the fish belly up and cut

through the ribs up against either side of the spine. Then with a sharp paring knife, free the spine. Discard the bones. Lay the fish on the counter on its side, and cut it across the back into 2-inch (5-cm) lengths—essentially creating a "saddle" of trout, or boneless steaklets. 3. Put the fish into a glass jar, cover them with onion rings, slide the dill sprigs into the mix, and pour the cooled vinegar marinade over the top. Refrigerate for at least 24 hours. Serve as an appetizer for a hot summer party.

Note: I know trout is considered a cold-water fish, but the water is not so cold that parasites wouldn't grow in it. Therefore, whenever you make any dish that does not apply heat until the flesh is flaky (sushi and this pickled trout are two examples), you must freeze the fish at 0°F (−17.8°C) for at least 48–72 hours to destroy any possibility of parasites. That freezer attached to your refrigerator probably isn't cold enough, but it's best even to check your chest freezer with a freezer thermometer to be sure.

Netting a rainbow trout in a Montana stream (Photo © Alan and Sandy Carey)

Blued Trout

Yield: 1 serving

This recipe should be called the Trout Two-Step, because it is one of the few fish recipes in classic—or even nouveau—cooking that requires two pots for one fish. When properly done, however, the results are striking. You need a very fresh, cleaned fish—no washing, scaling, lying in a creel allowed—of medium size (about 10 inches/25 cm). And while brook trout blue the deepest color, that slimy coating that makes any trout hard to hold on to is the most important ingredient in this recipe. So be very careful cleaning the fish you are going to blue, and blue it as close as possible to the stream. What I'd like to know is who was that first fool that set a pot of vinegar boiling, streamside, and discovered this char-oddity?

The First Pot Ingredients

2 cups (500 ml) dry white wine
2 cups (500 ml) water
1 onion, sliced
1 carrot, chopped
1 stick celery, with leaves
1 teaspoon dried thyme leaf
1 whole clove
2 bay leaves
2 teaspoons salt
10 peppercorns

The Second Pot Ingredients

Mix enough solution to cover the fish,
   including:
2 parts vinegar
1 part water
10-inch (25 cm) brook trout, very fresh

Cooking

1. For the first pot: combine the wine, water, onion, carrot, celery, thyme, clove, bay leaves, salt, and peppercorns in a large saucepan, and bring to a boil. Turn down the heat and let simmer about 30 minutes. In the meantime, combine the vinegar and water for the second pot in another saucepan. When the first pot is about ready, bring the second pot to a boil.

2. With kitchen tongs, grasp the trout by the jaw and lower it gently into the vinegar solution in the second pot. Do not release the fish. As soon as the fish is blue (it only takes a few seconds, and only the best brookies turn a deep robin's egg blue), remove it from the vinegar solution and lower it gently into the simmering first pot. When the bouillon returns to a boil, cover the pot, remove it from the heat, and let stand 15 minutes. Remove the fish carefully with a spatula or two, and serve with a traditional hollandaise sauce or Tarragon Mayonnaise.

Tarragon Mayonnaise

Ingredients

1 cup (250 ml) mayonnaise
1 tablespoon minced fresh parsley
2 green onions, minced
$\frac{1}{4}$ teaspoon dried leaf tarragon
$\frac{1}{4}$ teaspoon dry mustard
$\frac{1}{4}$ teaspoon salt
Dash of white pepper

Preparation

In a small bowl, combine the mayonnaise, parsley, onions, tarragon, mustard, salt, and pepper. Stir to mix thoroughly, cover, and chill 1–4 hours.

Sauer Trout

Yield: 12 servings as appetizers

I live near a string of reservoirs on the upper Missouri River, famous not only for its trout, but the zeal of its anglers. In the summer, the highways around here are full of boats; in the winter, pickup trucks sport the colorful bobbers of ice fishing. And spring . . . well, if the power company doesn't lower the lake at just the wrong time, the rainbow run is pretty darn good. The result is that the natives have a lot of really good ways to cook trout. This recipe is from the kitchen of Ruth Zimmerman, and it is one of our local classics.

Sauer Trout, a variation on the classic Sauerbraten without all the marinating

Ingredients

2 pounds (1 kg) trout fillets
2 tablespoons butter
$\frac{1}{2}$ cup (125 ml) minced onion
$1\frac{1}{2}$ cups (375 ml) apple juice
1 cup (250 ml) cider vinegar
$\frac{2}{3}$ cup (160 ml) brown sugar
$\frac{1}{8}$ teaspoon ground clove
$\frac{1}{2}$ teaspoon whole mustard seeds
1 bay leaf
$\frac{1}{2}$ teaspoon salt
$\frac{1}{2}$ cup (125 ml) crushed gingersnaps

Cooking

1. Cut the fillets into serving-sized pieces. In a large skillet, melt the butter over medium heat, then add the onion and cook until tender, about 5 minutes. Stir in the apple juice, vinegar, brown sugar, clove, mustard seeds, bay leaf, and salt. Add the fish, cover, and simmer 3–5 minutes, until the fish flakes.

2. Remove the fish to a serving dish. Gradually sprinkle the crushed gingersnaps into the pan liquid, stir to dissolve. The ground snaps will thicken the sauce, but—like flour in gravy—have a tendency to lump if added too quickly. Remove the bay leaf. Pour over the fish, and serve hot as a hearty appetizer.

Brook trout (Photo © Doug Stamm/ProPhoto)

TROUT LOUIS

Yield: 6 servings

I have a pair of expensive, midnight-blue neoprene waders that are too bright for waterfowling, so I must wear them fishing. And I read in my newspaper that people of any age should not wade wet in cold creeks on hot summer days for fear of creating or aggravating varicose veins. But give me a hot August afternoon, with thunder clouds building in the skies over the Elkhorn Mountains, and I throw both waders and caution to the wind. With a bit of Louis in the refrigerator and a creel of naive little pan trout, dinner is ready before the first rain falls.

Louis Dressing Ingredients

1 cup (250 ml) mayonnaise
¼ cup (60 ml) chili sauce
2 tablespoons grated onion
2 tablespoons minced parsley
Pinch of cayenne pepper
⅓ cup (80 ml) heavy cream

Trout Ingredients

6 pan-sized trout, whole
1 head leaf lettuce
6 hard boiled eggs, quartered
6 large, ripe tomatoes, quartered
Pepper, to taste

Preparation

In a bowl, combine the mayonnaise, chili sauce, onion, parsley, and cayenne pepper. Stir well. Whip the cream, then fold it gently into the mayonnaise mixture. Cover and chill (while you fish for six pan-sized trout).

Cooking

1. Rinse the fish in cold water, then pat dry with a paper towel. Wrap in a paper towel and microwave 60 seconds on high in a 500-watt oven, 30 seconds in a 700-watt unit. Check the inside of the trout for doneness: The meat at the top of the back will be opaque, but still moist looking. Remove the paper toweling and cover the fish with plastic wrap. Chill.

2. To serve, tear the lettuce and divide onto six plates. Flake the chilled meat off the trout and arrange on the lettuce. Garnish with egg and tomato quarters, season with pepper, and top with a generous spoonful of the Louis dressing.

Fly fishing in a float tube on Alaska's Auke Lake (Photo © Mark Kelley)

FOILED TROUT WITH CHAMPAGNE SAUCE

Yield: 4 servings

The truth is, I don't know if there is any one recipe for this classic dish. Look from cookbook to cookbook and everyone has a recipe to swear by. I use champagne, not because a simple white wine isn't good enough for my "elevated standards," but because good dry white wines are as rare in Montana as white rhinos. On the other hand, inexpensive dry champagne is as available as pop. A word of warning however: *sec* is the French word for dry, but in champagne actually refers to a slightly sweet taste. Look for the word *brut* or "extra dry" on the label for truly dry flavor.

Foiled Trout with Champagne Sauce ready to go in the oven

Foiled Trout Ingredients

2 cups (500 ml) *brut* champagne
2 bay leaves
1 ½ teaspoons dried oregano leaves
½ teaspoon dried thyme leaf
2 trout, whole, 14 inches (35 cm) long each
2 garlic cloves, halved
1 teaspoon salt
½ teaspoon pepper
1 small onion, sliced
1 lemon, cut into wedges

Champagne Sauce Ingredients

2 tablespoons butter
2 tablespoons flour
⅔ cup (160 ml) cooking juices from foiled trout
1 cup (250 ml) *brut* champagne

Preparation

1. To prepare the trout: Preheat oven to 375°F (190°C). In a blender or food processor, combine the champagne, bay leaves, oregano, and thyme, and purée 3–5 seconds until the bay leaves are coarsely chopped.

2. Rinse the fish in cold water, then pat dry with a paper towel. Arrange the trout side by side, lengthwise on a heavy duty length of aluminum foil large enough to envelope and seal the fish and their juices in. Rub the trout inside and out with the garlic cloves, then season with salt and pepper. Turn the sides and ends of the foil up to make a bowl, and add the seasoned champagne. Arrange the onion rings over the fish. Seal the foil around the trout securely, then rotate the package three or four times to coat the trout.

Cooking

1. Put the package on a cookie sheet and place in the oven. Cook about 20–25 minutes, until the fish flakes easily with a fork or the skin peels away easily. Lift the trout gently out of the cooking liquid, place on a warm platter, and cover to keep warm. (Beware of the steam when you first open the packet and do not burn your fingers.) Reserve ⅔ cup (160 ml) of the cooking juices.

2. To prepare the champagne sauce: Melt the butter in a saucepan over medium heat, stir in the flour. When the flour is thoroughly mixed in and turning golden, gradually add the trout cooking juices to the flour mixture, stirring continuously. The sauce will thicken quickly. Keep stirring and gradually add the champagne.

Now the sauce will be thinned out again. Continue cooking and stirring until the sauce is the thickness of good poultry gravy.

3. To serve, peel the skin off the trout, then lift each fillet off; place each serving on a plate. Pour the finished sauce over each serving, season with a bit more salt and pepper if desired, and a squeeze of lemon.

Note: Note the short cooking time on this recipe. This is where I differ from a lot of cooks. I prefer my trout firm, not mushy, and find that the biggest problem in cooking fish is cooking it too long. Of course, if you like your trout mushy, leave the trout in the oven 45–60 minutes.

Foiled Trout with Champagne Sauce ready for the table

CHILLED TROUT SALAD

Yield: 4 servings

My husband, John, is famous for his odd taste buds—from banana and Vidalia onion on rye at lunch to cold pizza and orange juice for breakfast. But when he decided to substitute a freshly caught trout for the ubiquitous can of tuna in America's favorite fish dish, the rest of us sat up and took notice. This is a sandwich anyone could love.

A fly fisherman works a trout in a Montana stream (Photo © Alan and Sandy Carey)

Ingredients

1 trout, 10 inches (25 cm) long
1 tablespoon sweet pickle relish
1 tablespoon diced onion
$\frac{1}{4}$ teaspoon garlic salt
Pinch of black pepper
Pinch of cayenne pepper
$\frac{1}{2}$ cup (125 ml) mayonnaise
8 slices toast
Lettuce

Cooking

1. About 1 hour ahead, catch and clean the trout and wrap it in a paper towel. Microwave on high in a 500-watt unit for 60 seconds, 30 seconds in a 700-watt oven. Test the fish: if you can't take a butter knife and slide the meat off the bones, microwave a few seconds longer. Don't overcook the trout, however: small trout microwave quickly. Take the trout out of the microwave and place in the refrigerator to chill, about 45 minutes.

2. When you are ready to eat, stir the relish, onion, garlic salt, and pepper into the mayonnaise. Then, flake the flesh off the bones and fold it into the mayonnaise mixture.

3. To assemble the sandwich, spread a bit of mayonnaise on the bottom slice of bread, divide the trout salad equally, then top with lettuce. Add slices of tomato, sweet Vidalia onion, or pimento, and garnish with a sprinkle of paprika if you want. Or avoid the bread altogether and stuff a ripe tomato with the salad mixture. Trout salad is as versatile as you want it to be.

SUSHI

Yield: 8–10 servings

The rule of sushi is to use only the freshest of ingredients; but the reality of trout water is that if you don't freeze the fish at 0°F (–17.8°C) for 48–72 hours you may have trouble with parasites. Don't let that stop you from trying this delicious classic Japanese preparation, but do buy yourself a freezer thermometer to be safe. And one more thing: You can make sushi without *nori*, but the concentrated salt flavor of pressed saltwater seaweed coupled with the intense heat of the mustard adds a delicious wallop to the trout—rather like the coarse salt on the rim of a margarita glass.

Ingredients

1 trout, 16 inches (40 cm) long or just large
    enough to fillet
2 cups (500 ml) cooked rice, cooled
$\frac{1}{2}$ teaspoon rice vinegar
4 sheets *nori* (sheets of dried seaweed)
1 teaspoon hot Chinese mustard

Preparation

1. Catch, clean, and freeze the trout immediately at 0°F (–17.8°C) for 48–72 hours. Thaw in the refrigerator overnight.

2. Just before you are ready to serve, fillet the fish, removing the skin and any small bones that remain. Cut each fillet in half lengthwise, then cut across the halves with a sharp knife, cutting pieces about $\frac{1}{2}$ inch (1 cm) wide. Cover and set in the refrigerator.

3. Put the cooked rice in a bowl, sprinkle with the vinegar, and toss with your hands. Then shape the rice into cylinders, about 2 inches (5 cm) in diameter and 1 inch ($2\frac{1}{2}$ cm) high and stand them on end on a platter. With a pair of scissors, cut the *nori* into 1-inch ($2\frac{1}{2}$-cm) wide strips and wrap carefully around the rice (like recapping a tire.)

4. Lay the raw trout chunks on top of the rice-*nori* cylinder, then dot with hot mustard. Serve immediately, by itself or with a table of appetizers.

Note: All sushi is frozen for safety—if prepared by someone who knows what they're doing. According to *Gourmet* magazine (October 1996), fish destined for sushi in Japan is flash frozen at –60°F (–51°C) or colder, minutes after being caught. Since even the best home chest freezer will not go that low, we simply need to lengthen the time the fish is frozen before consumption to destroy bacteria and parasites.

SALMON AND STEELHEAD

Salmon has what you might call a spotted past. The French loved it so well, they coined a word for their favorite part, the *mitan*, or middle of the fish. Native Americans of the Pacific Northwest chipped great cedar trees into planks to cook it. Indentured servants in colonial America had a clause in their contracts that their owner/employers not make them eat it seven days a week. Yet kings and queens, princes and paupers alike have poached, braised, grilled, and baked it to near extinction. Salmon were dammed from the Columbia and other great Pacific spawning grounds during the Great Depression, but today there is a movement afoot to tear down those monuments to human survival in the name of salmon survival. It is one of the few fish people will get on an airplane to go catch, and it's the only fatty food doctors encourage us to eat. And that's only the start of the controversy.

Depending on where you live and what your culture prefers to do with food, you will prefer different types of salmon. Some believe the red-fleshed salmon is best. According to *Larousse Gastronomique*, the dry and pale flesh is best. Yet, Inuits of coastal Alaska shun pale salmon, referring to pink-fleshed chum as "dog" salmon, because that's what they feed it to.

Perhaps it's simply the size that fascinates us: It's always the bigger animals of any variety that attract our imagination. Jerk a panfish out of the water and it's gone before you have much time to contemplate its place in the universe. Fight a 30-pound (13½-kg) salmon for 45 minutes, and you begin to contemplate *your* place in the universe. If you need a meaty topic to ponder while you reel in big red, begin with salmon's place in biology books.

Pacific salmon are closely related to rainbow and cutthroat trout. Atlantic salmon are related to browns. In fact, on the west coast of Europe, that other Atlantic seaboard, salmon aren't the only fish running upstream to spawn; seagoing brown trout do it as well. Now add two more fish to the chowder: arctic char and steelhead. Steelhead are also indigenous to the Pacific Ocean and are seagoing, river runners related to rainbow trout, but they live to spawn more than once—like Atlantic salmon. Arctic char are related to Dolly Varden and brook trout—all of them technically char—but have

flesh as orange and oily as any salmon. If you're out there trying to catch one, they are as different as their biology implies, but for the purposes of cooking, you need only refer to one section in the book. The taste is the same, whatever the Latin name.

Which gets us back to the cultural differences in preferences for salmon. They may not be as arbitrary as they seem. Just compare the water temperature of our own Pacific and Atlantic coastal habitat. Put a foot into the Atlantic, where the Gulf Stream washes the beaches from Key West to Cape Cod with warm, inviting water, then just try to walk into the frigid Pacific up to your knees. Suddenly all those postcards of millions of languid waders at Atlantic City, versus wetsuit-clad, surface-skimming surfers in California make sense. Multiply that by every coast, every major river delta, every country and ocean current in the world, and you see the problem with trying to define this wide-ranging fish: water may seek its own level, but there is no such thing as a constant temperature.

Depending on how warm or cold the water is, and, therefore what the fish eats, not to mention how far up the river you catch it, the flesh can vary dramatically—not only in color, but also in texture and oil content. Color varies from chum pink to sockeye/Kokanee red; fat varies from 46 percent in sockeye to 28.3 percent for chum. Perhaps Scandinavians are adept at smoking fish because the colder water makes the flesh more firm as well as oilier; research suggests that fish that live and forage in colder water have higher levels of Omega-3 fatty acids. And while oily, firm flesh is best for smoking, the Scandinavians haven't deforested their country for the benefit of their navies—and conquest—as other European countries have. Their waters produce fine smoking salmon, and they have the wood to smoke it. The rest is as individual as how much salt you put on your food, and where and what fish you like to catch. I assume that even some Scandinavians don't like smoked fish.

Last October I was fishing for walleye and pike. I was hoping the walleye would be in their fall habitat, but it turned out they were inbetween their summer and fall cabins. We took a pile of pike, a smidgen of sauger, a brace of gold eye, then turned back a few hammer handles and cigars (small pike and walleye, locally). I did a long release on a giant pike—a very long release—and still wish I could have just gotten a peek to see how big he was. Each morning we took off from the marina, slowly cruising around a crowd of boats that never seemed to move.

"Salmon," one guy offered, when we asked him what he was catching. In October? We ignored the trollers and their salmon, but at the end of the second day, the call of the big red tempted me beyond my will. We spent the last half hour of light trolling unsuccessfully among the other boaters in the marina bay. Ah, the allure. Until we went to the cleaning station. Here were grown men holding their noses while they filleted these giants of the deep, at the same time looking down those same noses at our prime pike fillets.

When it comes to game fish, sometimes the most important factor in what we eat is what we love to catch. It's up to the cook to make the most of our impulses, and if you are like my husband, John, the cook has no problem. Biologists have actually discovered that some of us have more taste buds than others and therefore taste more intensely. John enjoys stronger flavors, from hot pepper sauce to mustard-soaked sardines. He has even shared the First American delicacies of bison tripe and caribou eyeball. I, on the other hand, am not John.

I believe that means I have more taste buds per square inch of tongue than John, but don't quote me. It is enough to know that it is not simply a lack of adventure on my part—or a lack of discretion on his.

Since stronger flavors generally reside in darker, oilier flesh, if you don't like strong flavors, try to convince yourself to enjoy catching the paler salmon—or incorporate the salmon into cheesy casseroles and spicy dishes. If you don't like the oily flavor, grilling is a good method of leeching the oil out, as is smoking. And if you think you don't like smoked food (or simply don't like the intense salt flavor), first of all think back to what you have tasted. If it was "smoked" via a bottled smoking liquid, you owe it to yourself to try real smoked fish. I thought I didn't like smoked food until the first time I smoked my own fresh-caught trout. Bottled versus real smoking is like the difference between store-bought and homegrown strawberries. They're two different species. Smoked fish is the same thing. And of course if you smoke your own, you get to control not only the intensity and type of wood smoke, but also the salt and sugar content.

Whatever your taste bud count and personal fishing preferences, here are some classic salmon and steelhead recipes.

When preparing salmon fillets, trim the thin edges and run your fingers over the surface to check for bones. The hemostat from your fly vest or a pair of needle-nose pliers works well for pulling bones.

SALMON MOUSSE WITH FRESH DILL BUTTER

Yield: 4 servings

Mousse is almost synonymous with salmon. For the most attractive and easy-to-handle molds, you should use the boiled-gelatin method of preparation. The gelatin makes it a lot easier to unmold in one piece, and since most people only prepare mousse for company or special occasions, appearance is important. The taste, of course, will be delicious, even if you serve the mousse in a pile.

Mousse Ingredients

1 envelope (1 tablespoon) unflavored gelatin
1/2 cup (125 ml) water
1/4 cup (60 ml) fresh lime juice
1/4 cup (60 ml) mayonnaise
3/4 cup (185 ml) whipping cream, or nonfat
    yogurt
1 stalk celery, chopped
1 small cucumber, peeled and seeded
1/2 teaspoon salt
2 teaspoons snipped fresh dill
8 ounces (200 g) cooked, chilled salmon,
    shredded

A 35-pound (16-kg) salmon requires three people to carry it. (Photo © Mark Kelley)

Dill Butter Ingredients

3 tablespoons butter or margarine, softened
1 tablespoon snipped fresh dill
1/2 teaspoon dried mustard

Preparation

1. To prepare the mousse: Sprinkle the gelatin over the water in a saucepan and let sit until the gelatin softens. Heat the mixture over low heat and stir until the gelatin crystals dissolve. Let cool to room temperature, about 10 minutes.

2. Combine the gelatin, lime juice, mayonnaise, and whipping cream in a food processor or blender and blend at high speed about 20 seconds. Add the celery, cucumber, salt, dill, and salmon and blend another 20 seconds at high speed until everything is puréed.

3. Pour into a lightly oiled 4-cup (1-liter) mousse mold or loaf pan. Chill until firm, about 8 hours.

4. To prepare the dill butter: Once the mousse is in the refrigerator, combine the butter, dill, and mustard, and stir until well mixed. Cover and refrigerate 2–4 hours.

5. To serve, turn the mousse out carefully onto a platter. If the light coating of oil doesn't make the mold slick enough, dip the mold in warm water about 5–10 seconds, then turn out. Serve on toast spread with fresh dill butter for an appetizer or a cool summer lunch.

DEVILED SALMON SPREAD

Yield: 2 cups (500 ml)

For Christmas or New Year's, a Fourth of July party, or just something else to do with leftover cooked salmon, try this spread. Between the tang of the mustard and the rich flavors of the egg and salmon, this will be a favorite at any party.

Ingredients

1½ cups (336 g) flaked, cooked salmon
½ cup (125 ml) mayonnaise
3½ teaspoons dry mustard
½ teaspoon salt
1 hard-boiled egg, chopped

Preparation

1. If you don't have any leftover cooked salmon, you can quickly microwave some, frozen or thawed. For a 1-inch (2½-cm) thick piece of fillet, microwave about 2 minutes for thawed, 4 for frozen, in a 500-watt microwave; for 700-watt units, allow 1½ and 2½ minutes respectively. Remove from the microwave, flake and let cool to room temperature.

2. In a medium-sized bowl, combine the mayonnaise, mustard, and salt. Add the flaked salmon and the chopped egg. Mix until smooth and chill. Serve on crackers as an appetizer, or on a hard roll with dill pickles for a meal.

Note: To make the perfect hard-boiled egg, follow these easy instructions. With a pin, punch a tiny hole in the fat end of the egg. Then place the egg gently in a pot with cold water to cover, and bring to a boil on high heat, uncovered. As soon as the water starts to boil, turn the heat down so the water is just barely boiling, and start timing the egg to cook for 2 minutes. Then remove the pot from the heat, and cover for 15 minutes. Remove the egg from the water, and plunge into cold water to cool quickly. Store in the refrigerator.

Deviled Salmon Spread

GRAVLAX WITH MUSTARD SAUCE

Yield: 2 pounds (1 kg)

Whether you serve the gravlax on a thick slice of cucumber or smear it on that old standby, crackers, this salt-cured appetizer is a vivid reminder of why we fish. The salmon takes time to cure, but you can go out and play—all day, several days—while the salt works, and still look like a gourmet cook.

Gravlax Ingredients

2 pounds (1 kg) salmon fillet, skin on
2 tablespoons salt
2 tablespoons sugar
12 black peppercorns, whole
1 teaspoon dried dill weed
2 tablespoons brandy or cognac

Mustard Sauce Ingredients

½ cup (125 ml) butter or margarine, softened
1 tablespoon prepared Dijon mustard
1 teaspoon prepared horseradish

The graveyard shift on an Alaskan lake (Photo © Mark Kelley)

Preparation

1. To prepare the gravlax: Rinse the fish in cold water, then pat dry with a paper towel. Lay it out on a cutting board and, with your fingers and a pair of pliers, tweezers, or the hemostats from your fly vest, find and pull all the bones, large and small. Trim the rough and thin edges.
2. In a small bowl, combine the salt, sugar, peppercorns, dill, and brandy and stir. Rub two-thirds of this mixture on both sides of the fillet, then place the fillet, skin side down, in a shallow glass or plastic dish and rub the remaining seasonings into the skin. Cover the fish tightly with plastic wrap, pressing it against the fillet to seal, and place it in the refrigerator for 48 hours. Turn it over every 12 hours,

and baste liberally with the accumulating brine.
3. To prepare the mustard butter: Cream the softened butter in a small bowl, using a hand mixer. When the butter is light and fluffy, add the mustard and horseradish. Mix thoroughly and chill until ready to use.
4. To serve, drain the brine off the lax, pat dry with a paper towel, and slice very thin across the top. Place on dark bread spread with the mustard butter and a slice of cucumber.

Note: Since the salmon is not cooked, you need to freeze the fish at 0°F (−17.8°C) for at least 48–72 hours to destroy any possibility of parasites.

A salmon jumps upriver (Photo © Len Rue, Jr.)

PLANK-ROASTED SALMON STEAK AND VEGETABLES

Yield: 2 servings

These days you go to a serious kitchen store and pay a few bucks for a cedar plank to cook on. But plank cooking started with the Native Americans of the Pacific Northwest in a forest full of cedar. Cooks simply used what grew wild around them and developed a cooking method that not only added a touch of wood smoke to the dinner, but kept it moist in the process. You can do the same: Cedar and alder are the most popular woods for flavoring salmon, but oak, maple, hickory, and fruitwood planks will also give a delicate smoking flavor in your kitchen oven. Just don't use resinous woods like pine; they impart a bitter flavor whether you are cooking indoors or smoking outdoors.

Plank-Roasted Salmon ready for the oven

Ingredients
1 medium sweet potato
3 small red potatoes
1 green pepper
1 medium onion
2 tablespoons cooking oil
1 tablespoon red wine vinegar
2 tablespoons grated Parmesan cheese

$\frac{1}{2}$ teaspoon salt
$\frac{1}{2}$ teaspoon pepper
2 salmon steaks (or a fillet), 1 inch ($2\frac{1}{2}$ cm) thick
Salt and pepper, to taste
4 large cloves garlic, unpeeled
1 baguette (small French bread)
2 tablespoons butter or margarine

Preparation

1. Prepare the plank according to package directions: wipe the cooking surface with 1 tablespoon of oil, then place in a cold oven—the plank will break if placed in a preheated oven. Set the oven control on bake at 350°F (175°C) and heat the plank for 15 minutes. If your oven has a preheat control, be sure to set your oven on bake, not preheat.

2. While the plank heats, dice the potatoes, pepper, and onion, and place in a large covered bowl. Add the oil, vinegar, cheese, salt, and pepper, cover, and toss lightly. Set aside. Rinse the salmon, remove any bones, and pat dry with a paper towel. Brush both sides of the fish with oil and season with salt and pepper. (If cooking a fillet with the skin on, cook it skin side down, but still oil both sides. Peel off the skin before serving.)

Cooking

1. Remove the plank from the oven and center the salmon on the cooking surface. Surround the steaks with the vegetables, place the unpeeled garlic at the corners, and return the plank to the oven. Cook 50–55 minutes, or until a meat thermometer stuck in the thickest part of the salmon reads 125°F (52°C); the temperature will rise 8–10°F (4–5°C) after you remove the plank from the oven. You'll notice these instructions don't follow the 10-minutes-per-1-inch (-2½-cm) rule. That's because the plank not only doesn't conduct heat, but it absorbs it. The good news is this longer cooking time allows the salmon to absorb more cedar flavor without drying the flesh.

2. Twenty minutes before the salmon and vegetables are done, split the baguette, lightly butter the inside, and wrap in foil. Place in the oven.

3. Spread some of the cedar-roasted garlic onto the hot, buttered baguette, and bring the plank and bread to the table, or serve buffet style from the kitchen.

Note: Christmas party coming up and it's too cold to smoke the salmon yourself, and too expensive to buy enough to feed a crowd? Get the plank out, and fix yourself a lightly smoked, in-house appetizer. Just follow the cooking directions above, and leave out the rabbit food. Then serve chilled with prepared horseradish on crackers.

Salmon fishing in Alaska: A grizzly bear shows how it's done (Photo © Alissa Crandall)

GRILLED SALMON STEAKS WITH WORCESTERSHIRE-AND-BUTTER BASTE

Yield: 2 servings

I've known two professional chefs in my short life. One is my sister-in-law who studied at the Culinary Institute of America. The other took a less bookish route, serving apprenticeships with the chefs of queens and presidents, and ran a funky little Italian restaurant for his fellow fly fishing enthusiasts and others. Despite the differences, they agree on one thing when it comes to cooking: the simpler the better. And both prefer their fish plainly cooked with a baste of melted butter and Worcestershire. The more I talk to anglers who cook, at whatever level of competence, the more this simple classic comes up.

Ingredients

3 tablespoons butter or margarine
1 tablespoon Worcestershire sauce
$\frac{1}{4}$ teaspoon freshly ground black pepper
2 salmon steaks, 1 inch ($2\frac{1}{2}$ cm) thick

Cooking

1. Preheat a propane barbecue on high for 10 minutes, then turn down to medium high. Or start four dozen charcoal briquettes and wait 25 minutes. To adjust the charcoal fire, spread the coals to lower the heat; pile them up to raise it. (Or for a real treat while camping or even at home, prepare a hot wood fire in the fire ring or barbecue: alder is traditional for salmon, but if you can find chunks of cherry, this fruitwood adds a rich, mellow flavor.) The fire, on either grill, is ready when you can hold your hand at cooking level for just 4–5 seconds.

2. While the fire heats up, melt the butter in a small saucepan or in the microwave. Add the Worcestershire sauce and pepper, and stir well.

3. Brush the steaks liberally with the butter sauce and place them on the grill. Cook about 5 minutes a side, basting frequently. Turn carefully with a spatula or use a hinged grate to cook them. If your steaks are thicker than 1 inch ($2\frac{1}{2}$ cm), use the 10-minutes-per-1-inch ($-2\frac{1}{2}$-cm) of thickness rule—it's pretty accurate on a fire this hot. The fish is done when you insert a fork at the thickest part, twist, and the fish flakes but is still moist looking. Serve with grilled vegetables.

Salmon catch (Photo © Leonard Lee Rue III)

OVEN-BROILED SALMON FILLETS WITH CLASSIC MEXICAN SALSA FRESCA

Yield: 4 servings

For a taste of summer in the middle of winter, buy roma tomatoes and let them fully ripen on a window sill. Or make the fillets and salsa in the summer when the vines are laden with sun-drenched tomatoes. Either way, the salsa is a delicious contrast to the salmon.

Oven-Broiled Salmon Fillets with Classic Mexican Salsa Fresca

Ingredients

1 cup (250 ml) chopped ripe tomatoes
⅓ cup (80 ml) minced onion
1 teaspoon chopped dried cilantro
½ teaspoon chopped jalapeño pepper (more, to taste)
1 lime, quartered
1 pound (½ kg) salmon fillet, 1 inch (2½ cm) thick, skin on
½ teaspoon salt
½ teaspoon black pepper

Preparation

1. Two hours ahead: Combine the tomatoes, onion, cilantro, and jalapeño pepper in a medium-sized bowl. Squeeze two quarters of the lime into the salsa. Stir gently, then cover and refrigerate. (I make this salsa without salt, but if you need it, add the salt at the table to keep the tomatoes from getting watery.)

2. Preheat oven broiler and the rack 10 minutes with the oven door closed. Pat the fillet dry with a paper towel, then squeeze the rest of the lime quarters over it. Season with salt and pepper.

Cooking

When you are ready to cook, remove the rack from the oven and lightly brush or spray it with oil. Cook the fillets, skin down, about 4 inches (10 cm) from the broiler for 5 minutes, without turning. (This is one of the pleasures of thinner fillets: they cook completely without having to be turned.) Turn the heat off and leave the fillet in the oven, door closed, another 2 minutes. The fillet is done when you insert a fork into the thickest part, twist gently and the flesh flakes easily, but still looks moist.

GRILLED SALMON STEAKS WITH HOLLANDAISE SAUCE

Yield: 2 servings

With the bad rap raw eggs have gotten lately, I decided it would be a good idea to try the hollandaise sauce in this recipe with new-age egg substitutes instead of the real yolk. You've still got the butter fat, but no more egg fat. And while Julia Child might not like it, I prefer not having to worry about the volunteer beasties growing in commercially produced eggs. If you don't worry about food poisoning, use two egg yolks instead of the egg beaters.

Salmon steaks ready for the grill in a hinged barbecue grate

Ingredients
2 salmon steaks, 1 inch (2 ½ cm) thick
½ cup (125 ml) egg substitute
1 ½ tablespoons fresh lemon juice
½ teaspoon salt
Dash of pepper
5 tablespoons butter

Preparation
1. Rinse the fish in cold water, then pat dry with a paper towel. Let rest at room temperature while you make the hollandaise.
2. To prepare the hollandaise sauce: Place the egg, lemon juice, salt, and pepper in the blender. Heat the butter to boiling in the mi-

crowave or in a saucepan, until it is foaming hot but not brown. Blend the egg and lemon juice mixture at high speed for 2–4 seconds, then start adding the hot butter in a thin, continuous drip. Continue blending at high speed as you add the butter. Do not add the white residue at the bottom of the butter pan. The sauce will thicken, about to the consistency of prepared mustard, but not as thick as mayonnaise. If the hollandaise did not thicken, pour it out into a small bowl, then drizzle it back into the blender on high speed one more time.
3. While you cook the steaks, cover the blender bowl and set it in tepid water to keep the sauce from separating.

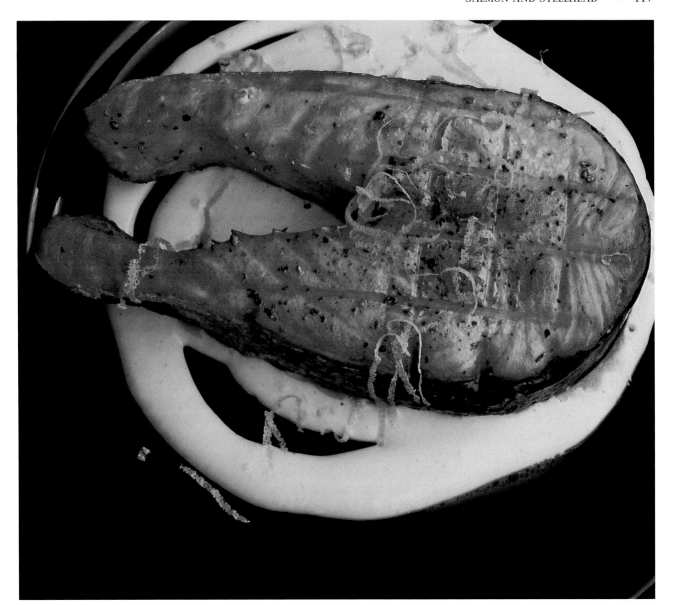

Cooking

1. Preheat a propane barbecue on high for 10 minutes, then turn down to medium high. Or start four dozen charcoal briquettes and wait 25 minutes. The fire, on either grill, is ready when you can hold your hand at cooking level for just 4–5 seconds. To adjust the charcoal fire, spread the coals to lower the heat; pile them up to raise it.

2. Lightly oil the steaks to prevent sticking, or use a hinged grate to make turning less hazardous. Place the steaks on the grill surface, and cook about 3–4 minutes to a side. The salmon is done when you insert a fork into the thickest part, twist, and the flesh is opaque and flakes, but still looks moist. Divide the hollandaise onto two plates, and nestle the steaks into the sauce. (You may need to purée the sauce 1 second, for it to pour easily.) Grate a bit of fresh lemon peel over the top and serve.

Grilled Salmon Steaks with Hollandaise Sauce

SIMPLE SALMON

Yield: 4–6 servings

The good news is you caught a great big salmon just in time for your friend's wedding. The bad news is now you have to cook the whole thing evenly all over without it falling apart. The answer? Aluminum foil. Use the heavy-duty stuff, and you can spin that big silver-wrapped fish like a top.

Fly fishing under the shadow of the Lewis River Falls in Yellowstone (Photo © Jeff and Alexa Henry)

Ingredients
1 whole salmon, 2–3 pounds (1–1½ kg)
Fresh ginger, 2 inches (5 cm) long
2 tablespoons soy sauce
1 teaspoon black pepper

Cooking
1. Preheat a propane barbecue on high for 10 minutes, then turn down to medium high. Or start four dozen charcoal briquettes and wait 25 minutes. The fire, on either grill, is ready when you can hold your hand at cooking level for just 4–5 seconds. To adjust the charcoal fire, spread the coals to lower the heat; pile them up to raise it.

2. In the meantime, prepare the salmon. Lay out a 2-foot (60-cm) length of aluminum foil on the counter. Rinse the fish in cold water, then pat it dry inside and out with paper towels. Set the fish on the foil. With a potato slicer, peel the dry skin off the outside of the ginger, then slice the ginger into a small bowl. Brush the inside of the salmon with the soy sauce, and top with slices of ginger and the black pepper. Seal the salmon in the foil and place on the grill.

3. Cook for 35 minutes, turning often. Insert a meat thermometer through the foil into the thickest part of the fish and remove the fish from the oven when the thermometer registers 125°F (52°C). The thermometer will rise 10°F (5°C) more degrees in the first 10 minutes out of the oven; the final temperature should be 135°F (57°C). Let stand 10 minutes before cutting.

4. Serve hot or chilled, whole or just the fillets. To remove the fillets for serving: lay the salmon out on a cutting board. Peel the skin off the top of the fish, from gills to tail. Then, with two spatulas, lift the top fillet off the fish and transfer it to a platter. Strip the spine off the bottom fillet and transfer it to the platter, too. The bottom fillet should lift right off the skin.

Note: It's the last few degrees of cooking that are the quickest. So once the meat thermometer reaches 110°F (43°C), whether indoors in the oven or outside on the grill, leave it in the fish and check it at 5-minute intervals. It is logical only if you accept that something cold cooks slower than something hot—and that it is much easier to add a bit of cooking time than to subtract it.

STUFFED SALMON IN PARCHMENT '90S STYLE

Yield: 4–6 servings

If you live in New York City, or have access to a large gourmet shop, you owe it to yourself to buy a length of parchment and make this the old-fashioned way. But, if you live where the salmon live, and like me, would rather stalk the wily salmon than the stacks of arcane and expensive culinary paraphernalia, talk your local grocer into giving you an unused grocery bag. A standard-sized paper grocery bag will hold a 19-inch (48-cm) fish and still have room to fold the end over. But remember, the size of the fish is limited not only by the size of the bag but also the size of the oven. Measure diagonally, like a TV screen. If your fish is larger than the one I used here, you can cheat by removing the head or cutting the fish in two, but do fold the end of the bag over to keep in the moisture.

Ingredients

1 cup (250 ml) fish stock or chicken bouillon
1 cup (250 ml) dry white wine
$\frac{1}{2}$ cup (125 ml) diced onion
1 stalk celery, diced
1 teaspoon dried thyme leaf
$\frac{1}{2}$ teaspoon salt
$\frac{1}{2}$ teaspoon pepper
1 cup (250 ml) whipping cream
2 cups (500 ml) dried bread crumbs
1 whole salmon, 19 inches (48 cm) long

Cooking

1. Combine the fish stock and wine in a large saucepan and bring to a low boil. Add the onion, celery, thyme, salt, and pepper and simmer until the vegetables are soft. Remove the mixture from the heat and pour in the cream. Stir until thoroughly mixed, then toss with the bread crumbs.

2. Preheat oven to 450°F (245°C). Rinse the fish in cold water, then pat dry with a paper towel. Lay it out on a cutting board or counter and stuff with the bread crumb mixture. Using toothpicks as skewers, tie the body cavity closed with light cotton twine. Lightly brush the sack's surface with oil, then place the fish inside. Fold the end of the bag over and secure the fold with two wooden clothespins or staple. If you have parchment, brush it with oil, then place the fish at one side. Fold the parchment over the head and tail, then roll the fish up in the parchment.

3. Bake the fish about 10 minutes for every 1 inch (2 $\frac{1}{2}$ cm) of thickness—measuring after the fish is stuffed. Insert a meat thermometer into the thickest part of the fish and remove the fish from the oven when the thermometer registers 125°F (52°C). The thermometer will rise 10°F (5°C) more degrees in the first 10 minutes out of the oven; the final temperature should be 135°F (57°C).

4. Scoop out the stuffing and place it on a platter. Now remove the fillets: lay the fish on a cutting board and peel the skin off the top of the salmon from gills to tail. Then, with two spatulas, carefully lift the exposed fillet off and arrange around the stuffing. Strip the spine off the bottom fillet, then lift that fillet off and place on the platter, too. Serve with fresh, steamed asparagus.

SALMON CHOWDER

Yield: 4 servings

This is a classic creamy New England chowder, but instead of reaching for all those expensive clams, serve up the rich, red sockeye or Kokanee salmon you caught last summer. Your wallet and taste buds will be a bit fatter for it.

Ingredients
2 slices bacon, diced
1 large red onion, coarsely chopped
2 cloves garlic, minced
2 cups (500 ml) fish stock or chicken bouillon
½ cup (125 ml) white wine
1 bay leaf
½ teaspoon ground allspice
1 teaspoon salt (reduce or delete if using
    commercial bouillon)
½ teaspoon pepper
2 cups (500 ml) milk
12 ounces (300 g) salmon fillet or steak
3 tablespoons butter
3 tablespoons flour
½ cup (125 ml) heavy cream

Cooking
1. In a heavy-bottomed soup pot or Dutch oven of 5-qt (4¾-liter) capacity, brown the bacon over medium heat until crisp. Remove the bacon, then discard all but 2 tablespoons of the fat. Sauté the onion and garlic in the fat over medium heat until they are tender. Return the bacon to the pot, then add the stock, wine, bay leaf, allspice, salt, pepper, and 1 cup (250 ml) of the milk. Bring the chowder to a gentle boil, then turn the heat down to a simmer, cover, and simmer 20 minutes. While the chowder slowly cooks, cut the salmon into 2-inch (5-cm) chunks, and gently drop them in.

2. Now prepare a white sauce: Melt the butter in a medium-sized saucepan over medium heat. Stir in the flour and when the flour begins to turn golden, slowly add the second cup (250 ml) of milk, stirring constantly. Turn the heat down to low and continue stirring until the sauce thickens, about 10 minutes. Do not let it burn or stick to the saucepan. (Microwavers, see the recipe note below for easy white sauce.)
3. Slowly pour the white sauce into the chowder and stir until it thickens. Add the cream, and cook just long enough for the cream to mix completely into the chowder. Remove the bay leaf, and serve immediately with oyster crackers.

Note: White sauce is not only a classic sauce, but a thickener as well. The trick, however, is that it has to cook long enough to thicken, but not long or high enough to brown or stick to the bottom of the pan. If you don't have heavy-bottomed saucepans, that becomes difficult to do. So try this microwave alternative: Combine the milk and flour in a 1-quart (1-liter) microwaveable bowl. Stir or whisk the mixture well to dissolve the flour, then add the butter. Microwave on high for 2 minutes, then remove and stir well. Microwave another 1–2 minutes, until the mixture comes to a boil and rises in the bowl. Stir the roux down. It should be thick now, like a heavy turkey gravy. If not, cook 30–60 seconds more, watching closely for the mixture to boil. Now use as above.

Fishing for salmon from a float plane in an Alaskan lake (Photo © Mark Kelley)

CHEESY SALMON CASSEROLE

Yield: 6 servings

The hot, rich, one-dish meal is not only a perfect place to use leftover baked or barbecued salmon, but the classic remedy for frozen toes and fingers. Prepare this one ahead of time, then when you return from a bitter cold morning of hunting Canada geese or standing quiet as a church mouse in a wet and rainy Texas tree stand, pop it in the oven. This casserole is also recommended for lazy Sunday afternoons watching the Packers defeat the Bears.

Cheesy Salmon Casserole

Ingredients

½ green bell pepper, chopped
1 clove garlic, minced
⅓ cup (80 ml) margarine
⅓ cup (80 ml) flour
2 teaspoons dry mustard
¼ teaspoon pepper

2 cups (500 ml) milk
2 cups (500 ml) grated Cheddar cheese
1 pound (½ kg) cooked salmon, flaked
3½ cups (875 ml) cooked elbow macaroni
    (1½ cups/375 ml uncooked)
1½ cup (375 ml) frozen peas, thawed

Cooking

1. Preheat oven to 350°F (175°C). In a large skillet over medium heat, sauté the pepper and garlic in the margarine until the vegetables are tender, about 5 minutes. Combine the flour, mustard, and pepper and stir into the sautéed vegetables. This will make a thick roux or paste. Stirring constantly, add the milk to this paste, ¼ cup (60 ml) at a time, without adding so much at one time that the sauce gets runny. At first, the sauce will stay pretty thick, but thins as you add that last bit of milk, and takes a while to thicken up again. Be patient, and work gradually at medium heat (turn it lower if you get nervous), until all the milk is incorporated.

2. Add the cheese to the thickened sauce, and continue cooking until the cheese melts, stirring constantly. Remove the cheese sauce from the heat while you assemble the casserole.

3. In a 3-quart (2¾-liter) casserole, combine the flaked salmon, cooked macaroni, and thawed peas. Stir the cheese sauce into the mixture and bake, uncovered, for 25–30 minutes, until the cheese is bubbling and the top is golden brown. Let the casserole cool 10 minutes before cutting. Serve with Kaiser rolls and baked apples for dessert.

Note: You can make this cheese sauce in the microwave, but the taste will not be the same. This rich white sauce and the roux necessary to make it, are worth doing the classic way—on the stove.

Working late: An angler fishes Oregon's Chicahomany Reservoir (Photo © Dennis Frates)

ALDER-SMOKED SALMON

Yield: ¾ pound (300 g)

The combination of alder and salmon is a natural one that has stood the test of time. But you don't have to smoke the salmon in alder: use whatever non-resinous woods are locally abundant. If you have copious amounts cedar or fruitwoods use that, even mesquite—in small quantities—if that's what grows around your house. Classic recipes may be rooted in history, but there's no reason they have to be mired in it.

Alder-Smoked Salmon

Ingredients

2 cups (500 ml) hot water
¾ cup (375 ml) brown sugar
½ cup (125 ml) coarse salt
3 tablespoons real maple syrup
¾ pound (300 g) salmon fillets
3 cups (750 ml) alder chips

Preparation

1. In a blender, combine the hot water, sugar, salt, and maple syrup and blend thoroughly. Let cool to room temperature. Meanwhile, trim the fat and thin edges from the fillets and remove the bones. Place the fillets in a non-corrosive dish that is small enough so that the fish is completely submerged in the brine. Pour the cooled brine over the fillets, cover, and refrigerate 12 hours, turning occasionally.

2. Rinse the fish in cold water, then pat dry with a paper towel. Discard the brine. Place the dried fillets on racks from the smoker and let air dry for 1–2 hours, until the flesh is tacky to the touch. The fillets are now ready to smoke.

Smoking

1. For an electric smoker, soak your alder chips for 30 minutes in water, then drain. Place 1 cup (250 ml) of the drained chips in the pan and slide them into the smoker. Turn the smoker on and wait 15 minutes, or until the first sign of smoke appears; in other words, preheat the smoker.

2. When the smoker is ready, load the racks, leaving 1–2 inches (2½–5 cm) of space between the shelves and individual fillets to allow the smoke to circulate freely. After about 1 hour, check the chip pan and add another 1 cup (250 ml) of chips; refill the pan again with the last 1 cup (250 ml) when the last is reduced to ashes, about 1 more hour. Three pans will give you a rich, smoky flavor.

3. Cook until the meat is opaque throughout, about 8–10 hours at 140–150°F (60–65°C). Ambient air temperature plays a role in how long the fish needs to smoke. On a 55°F (13°C) day, it takes 9 hours; cooler days, especially windy ones, will take longer; warmer days will require less time. There is no point smoking at 20°F (−6.7°C) and below.

4. Serve immediately with crackers, or store for later. Well-smoked salmon will store in the refrigerator for four weeks, or in the freezer for three to six months.

Netting a catch at the end of day (Photo © Bill Buckley/The Green Agency)

INDEX